CORNISH LIBRARY - FHSU

X

1789 0009 2043 9

P9-BVM-389

DUQUESNE STUDIES

Theological Series

3

SCRIPTURE AND ECUMENISM

Protestant, Catholic, Orthodox and Jewish

SCRIPTURE AND ECUMENISM

Protestant, Catholic, Orthodox and Jewish

Edited and Introduction

by

LEONARD J. SWIDLER, Ph.D., S.T.L.

DUQUESNE UNIVERSITY PRESS, Pittsburgh, Pa.

EDITIONS E. NAUWELAERTS, LOUVAIN

1965

230
S974s
1965

DUQUESNE STUDIES
THEOLOGICAL SERIES

Henry J. Koren, C.S.Sp., S.T.D., Leonard A. Bushinski, C.S.Sp., M.A., S.T.L., S.S.L., Leonard J. Swidler, Ph.D., S.T.L., editors.

Volume One—*Albert Dondeyne,* FAITH AND THE WORLD. XI and 324 pages. Price: $5.00 cloth.

Volume Two—*Peter Schoonenberg, S.J.,* GOD'S WORLD IN THE MAKING. IX and 207 pages. Price: $3.95 cloth.

Volume Three—*Leonard J. Swidler, Ph.D., S.T.L., editor,* SCRIPTURE AND ECUMENISM. VII and 197 pages. Price $4.95 cloth.

In preparation:
William H. van de Pol, *Anglicanism in Ecumenical Perspective.*
Henry Fries, *Bultmann—Barth and Catholic Theology.*
J. H. Walgrave, O.P., *Person and Society.*

Library of Congress Catalog Card Number 64-8867

All rights reserved
© 1965 by DUQUESNE UNIVERSITY

iv

ACKNOWLEDGMENTS

Sincere gratitude is due to Duquesne University, Pittsburgh Theological Seminary and the Howard Heinz Endowment for helping to make possible the seminar on ecumenism in which these and other papers were delivered. It is within the framework of the first two of these that the seminars have been offered to graduate students of both institutions and with the participation of faculty members from both. The third has generously undertaken to financially support the seminars, including making provision to aid the publication of the lectures. A word of thanks must also be said to Nancy Van Vuuren whose secretarial and administrative assistance helped make this year's seminar as effective as it was.

CONTENTS

PAGE

INTRODUCTION 1
Leonard Swidler

SCRIPTURE, TRADITION AND ECUMENISM 9
Albert C. Outler

SCRIPTURE AND TRADITION IN THE
THEOLOGY OF KARL BARTH 23
Robert McAfee Brown

THE MEANING OF TRADITION 43
John Meyendorff

THE MEANING OF SCRIPTURE 59
George Tavard

SOLA SCRIPTURA 75
Markus Barth

THE RELEVANCE OF OLD TESTAMENT
STUDIES FOR ECUMENISM 95
Roland E. Murphy

JUDAISM, SCRIPTURES AND ECUMENISM .. 111
Steven S. Schwarzschild

TOWARD A COMMON BIBLE? 133
David Noel Freedman

BIBLICAL THEOLOGY AND SCHOLASTIC
THEOLOGY 151
Anthony A. Stephenson

ABOUT THE AUTHORS 187

INTRODUCTION

In the ecumenical dialogue today, one of the central problems—possibly *the* central problem—is the authority or role of Scripture, or, in other words, the relationship between Scripture and Tradition and the Church. The heart of the problem does not really seem to be whether there is only one source for Christian doctrines, the Scriptures, or two, Scripture and Tradition (in the sense that there were things that Jesus said and instituted which were not written down, but merely handed on orally). For those dogmas which have no apparent scriptural basis, e.g. the Assumption, and consequently seem to demand another source of revelation—Tradition—often really are not helped by the second source, as Karl Rahner has so ably pointed out. In the case of the Assumption the "Tradition" does not appear until centuries after the apostles. This would mean that the earliest Christians who were eye-witnesses, or who heard from eye-witnesses, passed on this tradition of the Assumption orally for centuries without mentioning it in their writings or causing others to do so—which is a rather large supposition upon which to base one's faith.

But if the heart of *the* ecumenical problem is not "one" or "two" sources, what is it? It seems to me that it is the *magisterium,* the teaching power of the Church: can the Church's *magisterium,* under the guidance of the Holy Spirit, express truths not found in Scripture—although not contradicted by Scripture? Father George Tavard and other Catholic theologians of a like mind say no, that all dogmas *must* be in Scripture somehow. Yet, we cannot reject the infallible teaching of the Church, the *magisterium.* Hence, they insist, we must believe, pray and work so that some day we will be able to see *how* these dogmas are in Scripture.

On the other hand Karl Barth, giving a not atypical Protestant position, would reject the *magisterium* where its

1

teaching obviously does not come from Scripture. Although, he maintains, it is through the Church, tradition, confessional writings, etc., that we best understand the Scripture—in fact, it is really only from within this framework that we can normally understand the Scriptures correctly—the *magisterium* can be in error.

Father Tavard and many other Catholic theologians starting largely from Newman insist that there has been no past error in the doctrinal positions taken by the Church, but that there have been partial statements which are in need of development. The direction of the reasoning runs along the following lines: one must in the beginning be very cautious in deciding in what instances the Church has actually definitively committed itself. This is not such a simple task when one looks over the vast expanse of the two thousand years of Christian history, particularly in view of the wide variety of forms the structure of the Church took in these millennia—Hans Küng's book *The Structures of the Church* is instructive in this regard. After this difficult task has been accomplished in any one instance, the next goal is to ascertain just what it was the Church definitively committed itself to. To begin with it must be realized that every dogmatic statement is always a partial statement; this is basically true of any statement about life. If we are trying to express some *mediate* knowledge we have gained through an analysis of something, the statement is professedly partial. Or if we are trying to express some *immediate* knowledge gained from a direct, intuitional contact, as it were, the statement may be more encompassing than the analytic statements. But it surely will fall short of the reality described, and even then the statement's depth of meaning will not always be immediately obvious. One might take as examples analytic statements about a person's characteristics, abilities, etc., each of which would necessarily be partial, and even all together would not adequately describe the person. Moreover, the direct, immediate sort of knowledge resulting

2

from intimate personal contact would not only go beyond the total of the analytical statements, but would also burst the confines of any poetic statement or collection of statements. Now if all this is true concerning the knowledge of purely earthly persons and things, what of divine persons and things? Our knowledge will be *very* partial.

Added to the facts that our knowledge of God and his revelation to man is very limited and that any statement of this revelation will be even more limited is the further difficulty that later generations may not ascertain correctly just what was meant by such statements. To understand, for example, the doctrinal statements of the ecumenical councils and other acts of the *magisterium,* one cannot look at them in the abstract. They must be viewed within their historical context. For a more specific example, it is obvious to the historian that the conciliar statement declaring Mary the *Theotokos* was in no way intended to contribute to the building up of a Mariology, but was directed toward Jesus Christ and his being the God-man. But even understanding the historical setting out of which a doctrinal statement issued is not sufficient to grasp its central message. There is also the whole problem of the meaning of the language and philosophical categories in which the statement is couched. This of course is already a problem in trying to grasp the content of Scripture and, though to a lesser degree, doctrinal statements in the later history of the Church. Yet we of a "neo-scholastic" period, according to the researches of Father Schillebeeckx, seemed to have misread rather badly the Thomistic notion of sacramentality, for example.

Moreover, it is necessary, in looking at a past doctrinal statement, to determine what really is the Christian truth which in a partial way, in specific philosophical categories, in reaction to a definite set of historical circumstances, is being communicated. Surely in the whole sacramentarian controversy which gave rise to the doctrinal statement on transub-

stantiation the truth in question was that of the real presence.
The Church at Trent was not trying to canonize the Aristotelian categories of substance and accident—nor *could* she in
any fashion that would exclude the possibility of using other
categories to express the truth of the real presence. As it
happens the terms substance and species—*not* "accidents"—
were used in connection with the mystery of the Eucharist
long before the influx of Aristotelianism in the thirteenth century.

Counter-Reformation confusion often led to an obliteration
of this distinction between the truth conveyed and its vehicle,
or, to use Aristotelian terms, between the matter and the form.
Father Charles Davis once used an analogy that is helpful in
this regard, particularly when there is a history of rephrasings
of a doctrinal position—the birth control question being a
pertinent example today. He said the Church is like a man
who has a nut in his hand. What he really wants to keep is
the kernel, but he dare not throw away the shell until he can
find a way to get the kernel. Thus, when new information,
new circumstances, new categories, etc., permit the Church
safely to discard an older formula in favor of one that will
more adequately express the truth, she is like the man who
learned how to crack the shell without smashing the kernel.
The difference with the Church, of course, is that there seems
by the nature of things to be an unending series of shells.

Professor Albert Outler has elsewhere produced evidence
showing that the Ante-Nicene Church always judged heretics
on the grounds of whether or not they interpreted Scripture
in keeping with the tradition as it had been received up to
that time. If they did not so interpret it they were judged to
be without the Holy Spirit and, therefore, were really not
even reading Scripture. This conclusion was arrived at by
reasoning that the Scriptures were God's message to man
and this message could be communicated to man only under
the guidance and inspiration of the Holy Spirit—"No one

can call on the Father except that the Spirit prompt him"—
and this was tested by matching past and present Church
teaching, the *magisterium,* with the newly proposed doctrine,
which if not congruent was held not to be in Scripture.

If it is true that there was major agreement on the content
of the Christian message, then the first centuries might well be
an acceptable common ground for most Christians seeking
unity. But what about the period after the divisions between
the East and the West and those resulting from the Reformation and its aftermath? Where is the Church tradition,
the *magisterium,* which is the measure of orthodox scriptural
interpretation? Either one Church, one *magisterium,* has remained completely true, as both Rome and Orthodoxy claim
for themselves, or *none* has remained completely true. This
position would be acceptable to many Protestants, but not to
Roman Catholicism or Orthodoxy. Hence the central problem
is no longer so much *who* can interpret the Scriptures, since
most would agree it must be the Church (*magisterium*), but
whether the *magisterium* has made (or in the future will
make) any essential errors? Protestants would say that the
magisterium could, has and will in the future make essential
errors, whereas Roman Catholics and Orthodox would agree
in denying this, but disagree on where the loyal *magisterium*
is lodged, in Roman Catholicism or in Orthodoxy.

The need for maintaining the doctrine of the indefectibility
of the Church would make it difficult for Rome to accept the
Protestant position of the possibility and reality of essential
errors on the part of the *magisterium.* The problem is a genuine one; it must not be understood merely as representative
of a rigid conservative position trying to retain its power.
For relativism is an abyss that must be avoided. If we cannot
maintain some sort of continuity, then our faith is not really
divine but merely earthly, man-made, constantly re-molded to
fit man's fancy. The Holy Spirit is obviously then not the
spirit of the Church. Clearly an essential continuity of the

Church, an essential connection of the present with God's redeeming action of the past under the guidance of the Spirit must be maintained. But in what does this essential continuity consist? For the Catholic this continuity means that the Church, under the guidance of the Holy Spirit, has not committed itself definitively to any doctrinal error.

Protestants have countered with the suggestion that the guidance of the Church by the Spirit does not consist in preventing the Church from ever embracing an error, but rather in guiding the Church in such a way that if it did err it would be capable of righting itself, of renewing itself—just as God's chosen people of Israel did under the Spirit's guidance. This constantly being recalled to the path of righteousness and truth by the promptings of the Spirit would provide the essential element of continuity.

Another suggested solution, or at least partial one, attempts to deal primarily with problems like those raised by the solemn declaration of the Assumption, which, although apparently without real scriptural basis or early traditional basis, has nevertheless been declared by the *magisterium* to be a Christian truth. The Protestants protest that since this doctrine is not found in Scripture nor even the earliest tradition it *cannot* be declared a Christian truth. Otherwise the door is opened for any newly constructed doctrine to be declared *de fide* in the future: we have here plunged into the abyss of relativism. Therefore, it is suggested, it would be helpful to distinguish between truths that are essential for salvation and those that are not. It is obviously concerning the former that Christians must have certainty and it is therefore in their regard alone that the Church, the *magisterium,* needs and has the assurance of the guidance of the Holy Spirit. It is these essential truths that are subject to infallible doctrinal definition in the sense that the *magisterium* will be preserved from error concerning them. Concerning other non-essential "truths" the *magisterium* need not, and therefore has not, the assurance of the guidance of the Holy Spirit. These "truths" would not be fit subjects for infallible doctrinal definitions. The argument then runs that it would appear that the bodily assumption of Mary into heaven (whatever that exactly means) is in no way an essential part of the Christian message, as is, for example, the Resurrection. Therefore it is not a fit subject for an infallible doctrinal definition. Hence the "error" involved would not be one that destroyed the infallibility of the *magisterium,* but rather a sort of point of order error in thinking this "truth" could be infallibly defined.

Doubtless these two lines of thinking, in the stated forms, cannot be accepted by Catholic theologians. But these and all other serious suggestions must be dealt with seriously. It will no longer do merely to anathematize them from a position of authority or to attack them in a polemical fashion. They must be met on their own intellectual, theological level in an atmosphere of mutual respect and trust. In other words, what is needed in this area, and in all others, is an open discussion that will find out exactly what the problems are, face them squarely and try with *all* availabe talent to answer them, knowing full well that many false ideas will have to be winnowed out as chaff. This is what the lectures and discussions started four years ago in the seminar on ecumenism conducted by Duquesne University (Catholic) in cooperation with Pittsburgh Theological Seminary (Presbyterian) have been attempting to do. The general theme of the seminar this past spring, 1964, was Scripture and Ecumenism. It is particularly significant that of the nine papers delivered six of them in large measure focused their attention on problems revolving around the relationship between Scripture, Tradition and the *magisterium.* I hope that the publication of these papers will serve as a stimulus to further thought and research in this area and an inspiration to the continued spread of this open search for truth beyond the walls of these two institutions.

Leonard Swidler

SCRIPTURE, TRADITION AND ECUMENISM

by
Albert C. Outler

One rather intriguing way of trying to realize the remarkable significance of this seminar is to consider the fact that it is assuming that its topic is a viable one, despite the opposing fact that, formally speaking, both Protestants and Roman Catholics are committed to contradictory and irreconcilable positions which, again formally speaking, would seem to preclude fruitful negotiation—and have, for four centuries. The reformers of the late medieval church (from Wyclif and Hus to Luther and Calvin) were determined to have a court of appeal beyond that of the corrupted hierarchy of an unreformed church and they believed they had found this in the Holy Scriptures: their sole and sufficient authority (infallible and indefectible)—hence, *sola Scriptura*. Thus, they gained a vantage point from which they could denounce tradition, in *all* its forms, as patently fallible and man-handled. The Roman Catholics, in reaction, reinforced their traditional notion of the plenary authority of the *magisterium ecclesiae*—and came very near to identifying this, for all practical purposes, with ecclesiastical authority (specifically the papacy). We know now that the Council of Trent did not intend to disjoin Scripture and Tradition nor to set Tradition over Scripture in any absolute or categorical fashion. But there is no doubt that this was the way in which Trent was interpreted by the Protestants—and by a fair number of Catholics as well. And, in any case, whenever you postulate *two* sources of divine revelation, you have an unavoidable question about their relationships: precedence, subordination, co-ordination, super-ordination, etc. On the Protestant side, of course, the clarity of the *sola Scriptura* formula was clouded by the nagging perplexities of the *hermeneutical* problem that bedevils every

9

form of biblicism. *Sola Scriptura:* yes, of course. But Scripture *must* be interpreted. How and by whom? The classical Protestant answer—and one can only marvel now that anyone ever thought it valid—was to produce confessions of faith which purported to summarize Scripture and to serve as a *hermeneutical* canon. Not the least of the tragedies of the Reformation and Counter-Reformation era was the way in which two inherently unstable positions became consecrated by bigotry and thereafter served to reinforce the schizoid psychosis of western Christendom. Thus, the reformers committed themselves to the *sola Scriptura* as their chief bulwark against *traditiones humanae* (and, by their definition, *all* traditions were all too human). The Romans—both in the sixteenth century and predominantly until now—have adjudged the *sola Scriptura* as culpably heretical. It is the obvious referent in the anathema of the *Decretum de Canonicis Scripturis* of the 4th Session of the Council of Trent (April 8, 1546). That this view remains current is made plain in that wonderful old thesaurus of ultramontane Catholic theology: Canon George Smith's *The Teaching of the Catholic Church:*

> It is the custom of the Church to distinguish two sources of revelation, Tradition and Scripture, the former name being reserved for that body of revealed truth which was not committed to writing under the inspiration of the Holy Ghost but has been handed down through the living teaching authority of the Catholic Church. . . . The other source of revelation is Sacred Scripture. . . . The only certain guide as to the inspiration and canonicity of all the books of Sacred Scripture is the authoritative announcement of the Church. . . . The Church, therefore, is the authentic and infallible interpreter of Scripture. . . . These, then, are the two sources of divine revelation: tradition preserved by the living and infallible teaching authority of the Church, and Scripture, the inspired Word of God: sources of truth which the Church preserves pure and undefiled, and from

10

which she derives that divine revelation which she proposes for belief in all ages.[1]

Or again, in the new *Catholic Dictionary of Theology* (current enough so that thus far it only runs from "Abandonment" to "Casuistry" [Vol. 1, 1962]), Msgr. J.M.T. Barton is downright blunt about it:

> It is to be noted, in the first place, that Scripture is not the *sole source of revelation,* since, side by side with it, the Church recognizes also divine and apostolic traditions. Whereas William of Ockam had associated with Scripture as the rule of faith the doctrine of the universal Church, the reformers rejected the doctrine of the Church and held that Scripture was the sole infallible rule of faith. The Council of Trent was at pains to correct this heretical aberration.
>
> The Bible is not the *first source of revelation,* either in order of time or in the logical order. . . .
>
> Again, Scripture, as one of the sources of revelation, is not *superior to the divine and apostolic traditions,* which are no less revealed by God than are the Scriptures . . .
>
> Again, Scripture is *not the total and complete source of revelation,* since, side by side with it, there is another source, Tradition. It may, in fact, be claimed that Tradition is wider in its ambit than Scripture . . .
>
> Finally, Scripture as a source of revelation is *not sufficient in itself.*[2]

This essay was written in 1959. Moreover, the distance between it and the schema *De fontibus revelatione* submitted to the first session of Vatican II is negligible.

On their side, the Protestants have been well nigh unanimous in their avowal of the *sola Scriptura*—as a password for true believers, as a shibboleth against the Catholics.

Although somewhat curiously omitted from the Augsburg Confession (save by abundant implication) the *sola Scriptura*

---

[1]Pp. 28-31.
[2]Pp. 266-67.

slogan was written into the Formula of Concord as the primary source of pure doctrine and, hence, the basis of all valid Christian unity (Article I, *De Compendiaria Regula atque Norma*) :

> I. We believe, confess, and teach that the only rule and norm, according to which all dogmas and all doctors ought to be esteemed and judged, is no other whatever than the prophetic and apostolic writings both of the Old and of the New Testament . . .
> But other writings, whether of the fathers or of the moderns, with whatever name they come, are in nowise to be equalled to the Holy Scriptures, but are all to be esteemed inferior to them, so that they be not otherwise received than in the rank of witnesses to show what doctrine was taught after the Apostles' times also, and in what parts of the world that more sound doctrine of the prophets and apostles has been preserved.[3]

Even where they have deviated from it, this is the measure by which all good Lutherans ever since have measured their doctrinal rectitude—and others' deviations from this norm.

Every Reformed confession from *Helvetica Prior* (1536) to that of Westminster (1647) has articles or chapters (usually at the outset) which constitute carefully controlled variations on the theme of the primacy of Scripture. As Calvin himself put it in the *Confessio Fidei Gallicana:*

> IV. We know these books [of the Bible] to be canonical and the sure rule of our faith, not so much by the common accord and consent of the Church, as by the testimony and inward illumination of the Holy Spirit, which enables us to distinguish them from other ecclesiastical books upon which, however useful, we cannot found any articles of faith.
> V. We believe that the Word contained in these books has proceeded from God, and receives its authority from him alone, and not from men. And inasmuch as it is the

---

[3]Philip Schaff, *Creeds of Christendom,* III, pp. 93-94.

rule of all truth, containing all that is necessary for the service of God and for our salvation, it is not lawful for men, nor even for angels, to add to it, to take away from it, or to change it. Whence it follows that no authority, whether of antiquity, or custom, or numbers, or human wisdom, or judgments, or proclamations, or edicts, or decrees, or councils, or visions, or miracles, should be opposed to these Holy Scriptures: but, on the contrary, all things should be examined, regulated, and reformed according to them.[4]

The earliest version of the XXXIX Articles of the Church of England (1563) asserts in simple forthrightness that *Divinae Scripturae doctrina sufficit ad salutem:*

VI. Holy Scripture containeth all things necessary to salvation: so that whatsoever is not read therein, nor may be proved thereby, is not to be required of any man, that it should be believed as an article of the Faith, or be thought requisite *or* necessary to salvation.[5]

Article VII proceeds to affirm the integrity of the whole Bible and Article XIX defines the church in terms of the Word rightly preached and the Sacraments duly administered.

The Savoy Declaration repeats the *articulum primum* of the Westminster Confession, and all other "dissenting" Protestant groups have similar and self-consciously biblicist formulae in their founding charters.

This unanimity would have been even more impressive had it not been for the fact that although all Protestant confessions were professedly biblical, they obviously are not identical.

Between Roman Catholic triumphalism in its claims for the indefectibility of the Church—which never has and cannot err in its determination of what Scripture really means—and Protestant biblicism and confessionalism, there is a great gulf

---

[4]Schaff, III, 361-62.
[5]Schaff, III, 489.

fixed, and no conceivable bridge to span it. And this is the way things were until so recently that one ought rightly to be astonished at what has happened, in the last decade or so, to re-open the question and, therewith, a new, fascinating, baffling frontier in the current ecumenical dialogue. This, incidentally, is one reason why I regard this seminar as so interesting and significant.

The "weather system" in which these changes have been taking place is now widely designated as "the ecumenical movement"—a conveniently vague phrase that points to a kaleidoscope of men and groups in search of Christian unity, or at the least, some surcease from the anguish and shame of a militantly divided Christendom.

Elsewhere, I have argued that the distinctive genius of this *modern* ecumenical movement (and this before Pope John XXIII came along to confirm it) is its basic shift of starting point from previous projects on behalf of Christian unity.

What makes the present movement significantly different from its predecessors is its prior starting point: the acknowledgment of the *existing* Christian community and the fact of mutual recognition between churches which sincerely "accept our Lord Jesus Christ as God and Savior." Modern ecumenism begins with *the present fact of our unity in Christ,* with "the God-given union of Christ with His Church" (to quote a familiar phrase from "The Message" of the Lund Conference). This beginning point has allowed the positive recognition, by the separated churches, of the gifts and fruits of the Holy Spirit in the other churches—even when this recognition may include certain reservations as to the fullness and validity of the Spirit's work in those other churches.

The ecumenical movement has made it possible—in a certain sense, has made it necessary—for separated Christians to begin by acknowledging the Christian *koinonia* (community) which already exists among the separated churches, as the essential precondition for ecumenical discussion, worship, and expectation. At Edinburgh, in 1937, William Temple made the basic point that "we could not seek union if we did not already possess unity. Those who have nothing in common do not deplore their estrangement." But if we are willing to recognize this unity that we already have—and to confess that it is not of our own making!—we can then proceed to the ecumenical business in a far different temper than if we approach it with a question in our minds as to whether we can *find* a basis of unity with "other Christians" *where none now exists. . . .*

In this way, ecumenical Christians have begun by recognizing each other—and themselves—as included in that one community where Christ is Lord and the Holy Spirit is the resident power and wisdom of God—and this as the proper setting for doctrinal debate and the reduction of theological disagreements. *This initial mutual commitment provides the right atmosphere for ecumenical work.* The "insoluble" issues do not have to be, as obviously they cannot be, "solved" by a vote or a showdown. This feeling of real belonging—of being "members one of another" in Christ's Body—effectively brakes the inclination to attack and to defense. It helps to dampen the impulse to withdrawal and to recrimination when the going gets rough. Such a program rests its hopes in what God is doing to bring us together and what we may find to do in response and obedience to the divine initiative. This approach readily recognizes that the outcome of our common quest is likely to be quite different from what any one of us would now predict. It is likely to be different from what many of us would now prefer![6]

In this new context, many new exciting problems appear. But, even more important perhaps, many of the old embattled controversies become newly negotiable. Thus, at the Third World Conference on Faith and Order in Lund (summer of 1952), the Protestants began to recognize (almost as if it

---

[6]Albert C. Outler, *The Christian Tradition and the Unity We Seek* (New York: Oxford University Press, 1957), p. 24-27.

were a discovery!) the crucial role of "Tradition" in *all* ecumenical discussion. This led to the establishment of a Theological Study Commission on Tradition and Traditions, whose story is told in a brochure called *The Old and the New in the Church* (1961) and whose report was submitted to the Fourth World Conference on Faith and Order (Montreal, 1963) and published as Faith and Order Paper No. 40.[7] This project served as a goad and bafflement to lead at least a small number of Protestants into a major reconsideration of the role of tradition—and to a critical appraisal of the *sola Scriptura* slogan—which lead to a conclusion that has raised a small hue and cry in Protestant quarters wherever it was noted:

> The history of the Church has made the formal anti-traditionalism of the Reformers obsolete. To defy the accumulated traditions of the medieval Church in the name of the freedom of God and of the renewing Spirit, the Reformers could speak as though traditions were always consequent upon Scripture, both logically and chronologically, and as though it were possible to preclude the development of traditions by firm adherence to the Scriptures as both the source and the norm of Christian teaching. Such defiance makes less and less sense as the several Protestant communions themselves spawn traditions of teaching and of usage that are no more (and no less!). Scriptural in their origin and validation than were the *consuetudines ecclesiasticae* against whose claim to apostolicity the Reformers protested so vehemently. Examples aplenty from the history of Orthodox, Protestant, and Roman Catholic theology, liturgy, piety, and polity support the thesis that, for better or for worse, or for a combination of the two, traditions are inevitable.
>
> The "free churches" on the North American continent confirm this thesis in their own histories . . .[8]

---

[7]Cf also *Faith and Order Findings,* ed. Paul S. Minear, 1963.
[8]Jaroslav Jan Pelikan, *The Old and the New in the Church* (London: SCM Press, 1960), p. 36-37.

Along with the Gospel they transplanted many traditions characteristic of the European communions and cultures from which they had come. Their growing self-consciousness as churches within a new nation made them sensitive to the ambivalence of their European past and their American future. Some of them, in the name of the freedom of God and of the renewing spirit, defied their European traditions and acted as if it were possible to preclude the development of traditions in a biblically centered church. Still, they also began to acquire traditions of their own, sometimes exchanging one set of traditions for another, sometimes grafting dubious new traditions upon dubious old traditions, sometimes developing strikingly effective new traditions, both as fusions from the past and as innovations *in situ:*

> In the midst of this process of tradition-building many theologians have gone on repeating the formal anti-traditionalism of the Reformers. As a result, there is no tradition more tenacious than the tradition of *sola Scriptura.* Yet theological history has proved that *Scriptura numquam sola!* Theological historiography has furnished additional proof of this generalization that *Scriptura numquam sola.* Much research into biblical history has been animated, in the words of one member of this Commission, by a "primitivist emphasis on apostolicity which refuses to accept the exegetical authority of the ongoing Church or to recognize the weight of traditional precedents in the interpretation and presentation of Gospel, Sacraments, and Ministry." Despite this emphasis, such research eventually discovered that tradition takes chronological, if not also logical, precedence over Scripture, and that the deeper our historical study goes into primitive Christianity, the more pronounced the influence of tradition becomes. Theological historiography has, therefore, been obliged by the empirical data to accept these facts: the primitive Church expounded its Scriptures in the light of what had been handed down by and about Jesus Christ; the primitive Church interpreted

17

what had been handed down in the light of the Scriptures.
. . . Thus, theological historiography has been obliged
to modify, if not to surrender, the traditional dichotomy
between Scripture and tradition in the study of Scripture;
and it has also been forced to reassess the role of tradition
in the very Reformation whose case against tradition it
claimed to be espousing.[9]

We had already begun our work in the Commission on
Tradition and Traditions before we discovered that similar
reconsiderations of traditional notions about Scripture and
Tradition were going on in Roman Catholic circles as well.
Geiselmann's lifetime study of tradition, we discovered, was
nearing its conclusion—but it was not published until 1958
(*Die lebendige Ueberlieferung als Norm des christlichen Glau-
bens*) and it has not even yet received the excited and careful
attention it deserves. One of the happiest serendipities of our
work was that it led us to personal acquaintance and collaboration with Father George Tavard—who was working then on
what is still the best book in English on the subject: *Holy
Writ and Holy Church* (but this, too, was not published until
1959). In the further course of our work, we encountered
many other significant manifestations of the revival in Roman Catholic circles of new perspectives: Congar, Danielou,
Holstein, Cardinal Bea! These remarkable developments
seemed initially quite marginal in their influence upon the
general corpus of Catholic thought before the beginning of
Vatican II—but quite crucial thereafter!

It must be emphasized, however, that the work we were
doing in the Study Commission on Tradition and Traditions
was our own in the sense that it was a *Protestant* problem—
or, more precisely, it is a problem with a peculiar poignancy
for Protestants: viz., the identity and continuity of the Christian community and its message in and through the vicissi-
tudes of space, time, *and schism*. We were trying to find a

---

[9]*Ibid.*, p. 38-39.

way to maintain the primacy of Scripture, to be clear about the fallibility and entropic nature of all ecclesiastical traditions, and yet also to affirm the reality of a singular, transcendental Tradition identifiable and active in all the various epochs and segments of Christian history. In this, and many other ways, the whole area of "Scripture and Ecumenism" has become a vital issue in ecumenical theology—and the age-old intransigencies of the traditional impasse have begun quietly to fall away, on both sides. This development, more than any other single one, has reopened the ecumenical dialogue at the threshold levels of theological authority, theological methodology, theological verification.

This is why so much was riding on that debate about *De fontibus revelatione* in the first session of Vatican II (1962). I can still recall the thud of my heart when I first read the first text of that schema, originally drafted by the Theological Commission—and the anguish of Lukas Vischer when he wrote of it as *"schlimmer als Trient."* There is, therefore, no doubt in my mind that the struggle of November 14-30, 1962, will rank as the most critical of all the crises that Vatican II had to risk and weather. You know the course and fortunes of that debate as well as I do—and so I will not rehearse them now. But what has left me still baffled is the plain fact that Cardinal Ottaviani's draft was traditional post-Tridentine doctrine and differed from other conventional expositions of that doctrine only in its lack of subtlety. Even as we were astounded and delighted by the really great speeches of Cardinals Lienart, Frings, Suenens, Bea, and the Patriarch Maximos IV, I for one kept wondering how their views could be reconciled with the official tradition without explicit correction of that tradition and this, I had presumed and still presume, is out of the question.

You know, of course, the outcome. You also doubtless know—or know about—the revised version of the schema, *De divina revelatione,* which was prepared for and distributed to the fathers of the Council last fall but was not submitted for debate (and was rarely mentioned even in the gossip of Bar-jonah or the Secretariat for Promoting Christian Unity in the *Via dei Corridori*).

Certainly from the standpoint of the ecumenical dialogue, this new text is a decisive advance beyond the old—and it opens up several very important lines for further study and development. The *unity* of revelation is recognized, the primacy of Scripture acknowledged, the traditionary office and authority of the Church clearly affirmed. *Sola Scriptura in ore ecclesiae*—an admirable formula and one clearly within the range of coaptation with the Montreal formulas on "tradition, tradition*s*, and *the* *T*radition."

And yet—interested and heartened as I am by all of these developments—I rather strongly hope that Vatican II will forego the doubtful pleasure of trying to whip this schema into shape for final approval and promulgation in the form of a dogmatic constitution—for that, I presume, is the form it would have to take. We have already seen how arduous and protracted the effort was to produce that splendid constitution *On the Sacred Liturgy*. Again, we know how nearly mediocre the results may be when the bishops rush a decree through without ample debate and adequate expertise—as in the case of the *De instrumentis,* etc. We know that the *De ecclesia* is far from finished; that a proper statement of the doctrine of collegiality is going to take a lot more time—and maybe a miracle or two—before it is in its proper final form. The Protestant ecumenist may feel more or less neutral about the *De regimine episcopis et diocesiis*—but he remembers that it took two weeks of debate last fall and may need at least another week in the forthcoming session. As for *De ecumenismo,* there are the tantalizing rumors from Rome that chapters I-III have been greatly strengthened (as they needed to be, especially chapter III), but there remains that business about chapters IV and V—and it would take a blithe or innocent soul to believe that the Mediterraneans are going to go along quietly with these—which means more time, more ruction, more patient statesmanship by Pope Paul VI and the Council management. And then—besides all the schemata on the agenda that might very well be assigned to post-conciliar commissions (*if* collegiality is affirmed)—there is the famous omnibus, schema 17 (*The Church and the World*).

Pope Paul has good grounds for his desire to see Vaticanum Secundum conclude as soon as possible. But I simply do not see how they can possibly finish off what is already on the docket (even without *De divina revelatione*) in one more session without ruthless steamrolling and cloture—and yet this sort of thing would repudiate the spirit of Pope John XXIII's plea for *aggiornamento* and Pope Paul's demand for *renovatio*. Thus, it would seem to me, that a fourth session is unavoidable—but, by the same token, a fourth session ought also to be enough for now. In any case, it would seem to me more fruitful in the long run to defer debate on *De divina revelatione* or, at the very most, publish a yet further revised version in some programmatic form intended to encourage further study and reflection both within the Roman Catholic Church and among the separated brethren—and between the two!

The contemporary biblical renaissance in the Roman Catholic Church is still nearer its origins than its climax. What has already happened makes it more than probable that even more remarkable progress is yet to come (and this within the basic terms of Catholic ecclesiology. For, mind you, I'm not expecting, or even hoping for, Catholics to become Protestants. It will be quite enough for Catholics to become more and more evangelical, just as it will be quite enough for Protestants to become more and more truly catholic until some providential point of convergence is reached.

Over on the other side, the emergence of tradition as a Protestant theological problematic is still so recent that it has

hardly reached the generality of the professional theologians
—let alone the rank and file of the leadership in the churches.
But, again, what has happened already gives promise that
this is only a beginning—and that a genuine metamorphosis
could take place that would bring us far closer to the Catholic
sense of tradition than we have been since the hardening of
the lines in the sixteenth century. For their part, the Orthodox have served the dialogue by their dogged persistence in
expounding their notions of Holy Tradition. Thus far, however, they have manifested no perceptible impulse toward
critical self-examination—no disposition to review or revise
their traditionalistic views of tradition. One might think, however, that this is called for (maybe even prerequisite) if we
are to venture any further significant forward steps in the
direction of a fully ecumenical consensus about Scripture
and Tradition.

For all these reasons—and more—it seems to me that the
indicated program *now* is to recognize what gains we have
made, to encourage all ecumenical frontiersmen to continue
their work in biblical theology, on the one hand, and ecumenical historiography, on the other; and then go on, working and "waiting"—for *Vaticanum Tertium*. By then, unless
the spirit and sequellae of Vatican II are tragically stultified,
we may all be nearer that eschatological point of *convergence
into unity,* at the time and by the way God wills and grants it.
This working—and "waiting"—for that unity of Christians
which is yet to come is both a more realistic and also a more
responsible form of ecumenical obedience than any further
talk of "return" or any further bolstering of the defenses of
our mutually beleaguered citadels!

SCRIPTURE AND TRADITION IN THE THEOLOGY OF KARL BARTH*

by
Robert McAfee Brown

Of all Protestant theologians on the contemporary scene, Karl Barth has taken Scripture with greatest seriousness, and he has thereby been forced to deal with the problem of Scripture and tradition with greatest fullness.

Barth is ecumenically important not only because Hans Küng has written a book about him, nor even because he may succeed in writing more words than St. Thomas Aquinas, but also because he has genuinely tried to reclaim a *distinctively* Christian faith for our day. When one reads his massive twelve volumes of *Church Dogmatics,* now well over six million words, one does not feel a sense of oppressiveness but of liberation. One is not trapped within "Barth's system," but released from any system—liberated to take seriously and yet joyfully the central affirmations of the gospel. If Barth emerges as the great heretic of our day, it will not be for emphasizing the dark side of the gospel (as was true of so many of his Calvinistic forebears), but precisely for being (if such a thing is really possible for a Christian) too hopeful.

I. The Central Christological Fact

Here is a man who really believes that something quite monumental happened back in the first century, and that it

---

*The following analysis draws mainly upon Barth, *Church Dogmatics,* I/2, T. and T. Clark, Edinburgh, 1956, pp. 457-740, 743-884; *Credo,* Scribners, New York, 1961, esp. pp. 173-203; and *The Knowledge of God and the Service of God,* Scribners, New York, 1939, *passim.* See also Barth's most recent statement of theological methodology, *Evangelical Theology,* Holt, Rinehart and Winston, New York, 1963, esp. Part I.

makes all the difference. The Christian message is that *God is for us;* that he has declared himself on our behalf; that he has taken what Barth calls "the journey of the Son of God into the far country" so that we might know, once and for all, what his disposition is on our behalf, namely that he loves us unconditionally; and that in Jesus Christ he has declared and enacted this love and grace. To be sure, there are powers and forces of evil at work in the world, but there is nothing more powerful than the grace of God. Indeed, in his latest and twelfth volume (which has the barbarous subtitle, "Volume Four, Part Three, Second Half") he says that it is not enough to talk of "the triumph of grace," for that sounds too impersonal. The way we must characterize the message of the gospel is with the words, "Jesus is Victor" (a phrase adopted from the Blumhardts)—victor over sin, over death, over all that could possibly threaten us.

Secure at that point, Barth does not find himself confined and tied down, but liberated and freed to look at absolutely everything else in the light of that one blazing fact. *Creation* can be accepted and enjoyed as the arena, the theatre, in which this divine drama of victory has been enacted. *Men* can be seen not as dust destined for extinction but as those for whom Christ made the long journey, so that he could lift them up with him into the presence of the father. *Sin* we have always with us, but in the light of the conviction that "Jesus is Victor" it cannot be taken with final seriousness, only with provisional seriousness. *The life of the Christian* is the life of gratitude, the life of joyful obedience, of glad thanksgiving, in which, as Barth says, *charis* can only lead to *eucharistia,* grace can only lead to gratitude. So it goes for volume after volume; secure at this central point—Christ as Alpha and Omega, as beginning and end—Barth can see everything afresh in the light of this fact.

Including Scripture and tradition. . . . The old Protestant orthodoxies until recently were imprisoned within Scripture.

Roman Catholicism, it could be argued, until recently was imprisoned within tradition. Barth is imprisoned within neither; rather, he is freed by both, freed for the gospel which comes to us through the agency of Scripture and through the channel of the church that brings Scripture to us. We are beholden to *tradition* as it explicates the meaning of Scripture for us, and we are beholden to *Scripture* as it sets forth the nature of what God has done.

This means that Barth can take tradition more seriously than any contemporary Protestant thinker has done, and yet not be constricted by it. One never finds him repeating the old orthodoxy simply because the tradition sanctions it. While he aligns himself at many points with the old orthodoxy, notably in his claims about the nature of the virgin birth and the resurrection, he also displays a remarkable freedom from it whenever that freedom is necessitated by his allegiance to the Word of God mediated through Scripture.

II. *The Authority of Scripture*

In order to clarify Barth's position on tradition, it is necessary to say something about his doctrine of Scripture.

Barth has been called every name in the book on this matter. Critics on the left accuse him of "Biblicism" (whatever that means), and assert that he is so tied down to the Bible that he really lives in a private world of conventional orthodoxy where the air is stale and where there is no contact with living, breathing, twentieth-century man. But Barth is also under attack from the right, from those thinkers who find him even more dangerous than Nels Ferré finds Paul Tillich —and Ferré finds Tillich more dangerous than Father Tavard does. These critics find Barth dangerous because he "sounds" orthodox, but really isn't. He seems to be saying many orthodox things, they argue, but because he denies verbal in-

25

spiration and infallibility to the biblical text, he has really sold orthodoxy down the river.

We need to locate Barth somewhere in the midst of this crossfire. From the conservative critics let us learn that Barth is no fundamentalist, that he gives ample recognition to error within the biblical text, and that he is no enemy whatever of higher criticism, from which, indeed, he profits all through the exegetical portions of the *Dogmatics*. For Barth, in fact, it is extremely important that the Bible comes to us in intensely human form. God uses the biblical writers precisely as human beings. As he puts it:

> Every time we turn the Word of God into an infallible biblical word of man or the biblical word of man into an infallible Word of God we resist that which we ought never to resist, i.e. the truth of the miracle that here fallible men speak the Word of God in fallible human words. . . . To the bold postulate that if their word is to be the Word of God they must be inerrant in every word, we oppose the even bolder assertion, that according to the scriptural witness about man, which applies to them too, they can be at fault in any word, and have been at fault in every word, and yet according to the same scriptural witness, being justified and sanctified by grace alone, they have still spoken the Word of God in their fallible and erring human word.[1]

In other words, God works through the human text, for "the fallible and faulty human word is as such used by God and has to be received and heard in spite of its human fallibility."[2]

How are we to know that these fallible pages are the Word of God? Here Barth finds himself in the same kind of circle in which all Protestants find themselves, though Protestants would assert that the circle need not be a vicious one. Unless we are prepared to vindicate the authority of the Bible by

---

[1]*Church Dogmatics,* I/2, pp. 529-530.
[2]*Ibid.,* p. 533.

some authority external to it (such as an infallible church), thereby making *it* the ultimate authority, Protestants are placed in the position in which Barth finds himself placed, namely that the Bible's message to us is finally *self*-authenticating, and cannot be authenticated by any other norm. In typical fashion, Barth comments:

> The Bible must be known as the Word of *God* if it is to be *known* as the Word of God. The doctrine of Holy Scripture in the Evangelical Church is that this logical circle is the circle of self-asserting, self-attesting truth into which it is equally impossible to enter as it is to emerge from it: the circle of our freedom which as such is also the circle of our captivity.[3]

And again:

> For the statement that the human word of the Bible is the Word of God we can obviously give only a single and incomparable basis. This is that it is true. This basis either exists of itself or not at all. It is either already known and acknowledged or it is not accepted.[4]

I confess that I am always initially a little irritated by this kind of remark until I realize that there is no alternative to this kind of remark which does not bind us to a *securitas* achieved on human terms, in which we finally make something binding on God. That is to say, the alternative to the position Barth sketches is to find a way of proving the case by some humanly constructed device. We will believe the Bible to be the Word of God, for example, because we can demonstrate that it has no errors and therefore must be accepted. Or we will believe the Bible to be the Word of God because a group of people with very persuasive credentials tell us it is. In either case, this becomes for the Protestant a kind of idolatry. Perhaps, after all, Barth is finally right

---

[3]*Ibid.,* p. 535.
[4]*Ibid.,* pp. 535-536.

when he says, "The Church does not have to accredit [Scripture], but again and again it has to be accredited by it."[5]

A basic decision is made at this point. Either the Bible occupies a unique status, or implicitly some co-ordinate authority is introduced alongside of it, which finally rises up, Barth would believe, to smother it and replace it. The decision of the church to set itself under Scripture remains the valid Reformation decision.

As Barth develops this doctrine of the authority of Scripture in his later writings, it becomes clearer and clearer that Scripture does not exist simply to witness to itself. In later volumes of the *Dogmatics* the term "Word of God" (so popular in Volumes I/1 and I/2) tends to be replaced by explicitly Christological terms, so that any possible ambiguity is removed. The Word of God is not basically the words of a book; the Word of God is Jesus Christ, the Word made flesh. Scripture is so central for the church because Scripture is what Barth calls "the primary sign of revelation." But we are not to go back *to* a book, we are to go back *through* the book, to the One to whom the book basically witnesses, namely the God who has revealed himself in Jesus Christ. It is to bring us to him that the book is so necessary, for we cannot get to him apart from the book.

> The fact that the primary sign of revelation, the existence of the prophets and apostles, is for the Church book and letter, does not rob it of its force as witness. If the book rises and the letter speaks, if the book is read and the letter understood, then with them the prophets and apostles and He of whom they testify rise up and meet the Church in a living way. It is not the book and letter, but the voice of the men apprehended through the book and letter, and in the voice of these men the voice of Him who called them to speak, which is authority in the Church.[6]

---

[5]*Ibid.*, p. 536.
[6]*Ibid.*, p. 581.

So even Scripture itself is only a sign—but it is the indispensible sign, the primary sign, the sign without which the church cannot be the church. If the church, Barth says, "would see Jesus Christ, it is directed and bound to Holy Scripture."[7]

Thus if the critics on the left want to insist that Barth takes his stand squarely on Scripture, they certainly have a point. That he will admit nothing into the understanding of the Christian faith that is not grounded in Scripture or cannot be consistently derived from the revelation of God found in Scripture—all this must be admitted. But that this makes him a "Biblicist," in the pejorative sense in which that term is usually used, does not follow. Few men have taken with such radical seriousness the fact that if we are to know God we must look at the place where he gave himself to be known, namely in the Incarnation, access to which is cut off for us if we deny Scripture a normative place. And if Barth is right, as at this central point he seems to be, then any attempt on our part to take seriously the promises and the demands of biblical faith must align itself not too far from him in his concern to call the church once again to be *the listening church,* the church that hears what God has said and done, before it attempts to be the speaking and teaching church.

III. *The Place of Tradition in the Light of Scripture*

This raises, immediately, the question of tradition. The church listens, and then the church speaks. Its speaking is its "traditioning," its handing on, of what it hears. But a long time has passed since God acted in Jesus Christ on what Barth calls "the narrow strip of human history." By what critical standard is the traditioning process across those intervening centuries to be measured?

Barth had come to a fairly clear answer to this question as

---

[7] *Ibid.,* p. 583.

early as 1935, and dealt with the question of the relation of dogmatics to tradition in answer to questions posed for him by the Dutch clergy after he had given a series of lectures to them on the Apostles Creed.[8]

Understanding "tradition" as "the sum total of the voices of the Fathers," Barth immediately repudiates the notion that this could be a second source of revelation, this being for him the historic Roman Catholic heresy that must be avoided. (Discussions at the first session of Vatican Council II on *De Fontibus Revelationis* would suggest that the Council fathers likewise wish to avoid such a conclusion.) Rather, in order to avoid what becomes the self-apotheosis of the church, "the Reformation Scripture-principle placed the Church *permanently* under the authority of the prophetic-apostolic Bible-Word."[9] *"Tradition,"* Barth goes on to assert in italics, *"is not revelation."*[10] He also points out that this does not mean jumping over the intervening nineteen centuries "to the Bible alone," as the orthodox thinkers of the eighteenth and nineteenth centuries tried to do.

> These determined "Biblicists" had their contemporary philosophy in their heads, took it with them to the Bible and so most certainly read themselves into the Bible no less than Church Fathers and Scholastics. They were no doubt free of Church dogma but not of their own dogmas and conceptions.[11]

Far better, Barth seems to be arguing, that we approach the Bible in the light of what the Church has thought about it than that we approach the Bible simply in the light of what contemporary philosophy says about something else. (One can see, back in 1935, the terms in which, two decades later, Barth will be taking issue with Bultmann.) The Bible must

---

[8]Barth, *Credo,* Scribners, New York, 1936, recently republished in paperback.
[9]*Ibid.,* p. 180.
[10]*Ibid.*
[11]*Ibid.,* pp. 180-181.

be read by the church. We cannot ignore what the church has said, even though we must not apotheosize it. In a vivid image, Barth continues:

> To my mind the whole question of tradition falls under the Fifth Commandment: Honour father and mother! Certainly that is a limited authority; we have to obey God more than father and mother. But we have also to obey father and mother. . . . There is no question of bondage and constraint. It is merely that in the church the same kind of obedience as, I hope, you pay to your father and mother, is demanded of you towards the Church's past, towards the "elders" of the Church.[12]

In the selective process of dealing with the affirmations of the "elders of the Church," the norm, the standard, is clear:

> The norm that determines our choice is Holy Scripture. Holy Scripture is the object of our study, and at the same time the criterion of our study, of the Church's past. As I read the writings of the "Fathers," the witness of Holy Scripture stands continually before my eyes; I accept what interprets this witness to me; I reject what contradicts it. So a choice is actually made, certainly not a choice according to my individual taste, but according to my knowledge of Holy Scripture.[13]

This is not a matter that Barth has developed only as a principle. He has followed through on this criterion of selection in all of his subsequent writings, and it will be instructive to examine two examples of his attempt to do this: his treatment of the doctrine of election, and his attitude toward "church confessions."

A. THE DOCTRINE OF ELECTION

Here is an interesting example of the way in which the relationship of Scripture and tradition is developed by Barth.

---

[12]*Ibid.*, p. 181.
[13]*Ibid.*, p. 183.

In approaching a systematic setting forth of this doctrine, Barth, as a Reformed theologian, had expected to engage in a fairly conventional restatement of the traditional Calvinist position. As he put it in the preface to his volume on election:

> I would have preferred to follow Calvin's doctrine of predestination much more closely, instead of departing from it so radically. . . . But I could not and cannot do so. *As I let the Bible itself speak to me on these matters, as I meditated upon what I seemed to hear, I was driven irresistibly to reconstruction.* . . . It is because of the rather critical nature of the case that I have had to introduce into this half-volume such long expositions of some Old and New Testament passages.[14]

In other words, as Barth looked at his own theological tradition, and as he looked at Scripture, he saw a contradiction. He did not believe that what he read in Calvin on this matter was what he read in Scripture. (Let it be recorded that he is not the first person who has had this difficulty.) One source of difficulty, he felt, was the wrongness of the starting point of traditional theology. The starting point was too often some abstract notion of the omniscience or omnipotence of deity, from which certain logical conclusions were held to follow.

For Barth, this is wrong theological methodology. Christian theology, he asserts, can never move from the abstract to the concrete; it must begin and end with the concrete, the specific. If it wants to talk about God, it must begin at the specific point where God has shown us who he is, namely in Jesus Christ. It must begin, in other words, with the God who has declared himself for us, and anything it says about election must proceed from the basic fact that *that* is the kind of God with whom we have to deal, namely that Jesus Christ is the electing God, who has sought us in love. And when one starts with the biblical contention that God is for us, that God has elected us in Christ from the foundation of the world

---

[14]*Church Dogmatics,* II/2, p. x, italics added.

(Ephesians 1:4), then very different consequences follow from those that follow upon the conventional abstract starting point.

This is not the place to spell out all the implications that follow from such a starting point. All that can be stressed is that Barth's re-formulation follows from his attempt to take seriously the full impact of the *biblical* revelation as that revelation focusses in Christ, and engage in whatever re-assessing of the *tradition* may thereby be made necessary. As a result, predestination is no longer a question of incomprehensible darkness, as it was for Calvin, but of incomprehensible light. It is not a question of an absolute decree, but of divine grace. It is not a question of consigning so many people to eternal perdition, but of recognizing that Christ desireth not the death of a sinner. It is a message of hope, pure hope; it is gospel, good news.

Barth will not accept the tag of "universalist." He insists that if the old orthodoxy was wrong to assert that most men must be damned, it would be equally improper for us to assert that all men must be saved. But it is nevertheless clear to him that there is one thing that is stronger than man's demonry, and that is God's grace, and that those who *are* called are called to acquaint the "others" with the fact that God's grace is for them too. No man, he says, who has been the recipient of God's grace can deny that it is in principle available to every other man. Certainly there is judgment, but the fact is that the judge himself has taken our place, borne the penalty, cancelled out the debt. And to those who keep insisting that somebody must burn forever, Barth apostrophizes:

> Peculiar Christendom, whose most pressing problem seems to consist in this, that God's grace in this direction should be too free; that hell, instead of being amply populated, might one day perhaps be found to be empty![15]

[15]*Die Botschaft von der freien Gnade Gottes,* Evangelischer Verlag AG, Zollikon-Zurich, 1947, p. 8.

Against the logic-chopping of Calvin, and particularly the later Calvinist tradition, Barth is a liberating voice, simply because he tries to take seriously as his starting point the biblical affirmation that the reconciling act of God in Christ has actually taken place. The principalities and powers have been vanquished, for Christ has come. Jesus is Victor. As he put it to his students, speaking about Christology in the rubble at Bonn only a year after the war ended:

> Here we are standing at the centre. And however high and mysterious and difficult everything we want to know might seem to us, yet we may also say that this is just where everything becomes quite simple, quite straightforward, quite childlike. Right here in this centre, in which as a Professor of Systematic Theology I must call to you, "Look! This is the point now! Either knowledge or the greatest folly!"—here I am in front of you, like a teacher in Sunday School facing his kiddies, who has something to say which a mere four-year-old can really understand. "The world was lost, but Christ was born, rejoice, O Christendom!"[16]

B. THE PLACE OF CHURCH CONFESSIONS

The nature of the biblical affirmation, then, determines what is to be done with subsequent tradition. Let us now see how Barth develops this point in terms of certain specific confessional statements of the past.

Barth has given a great deal of faithful attention to the previous confessions of faith of the church. His concern with Scripture does not lead him to try to bypass the intervening nineteen centuries. He reminds us that our approach to Scripture today is partly molded and influenced by our Christian heritage, and we must not try to assume that this is not so. We must listen to what the church fathers have told us,

---

[16]*Dogmatics in Outline,* Harpers, New York, 1959, pp. 66-67.

and what the church, in various places, has tried to offer us as a compendium of the faith, a guide to the meaning of Jesus Christ for the contemporary moment.

Barth has written, for example, three books giving expositions of the Apostles Creed.[17] He has also given two series of lectures expounding the content of the Heidelberg Catechism.[18] But his most ambitious attempt to deal with a given confession of faith is found in his Gifford Lectures for 1937-38, given at the University of Aberdeen, and structured in the form of a long running commentary on the Scots Confession of 1560.[19] We can use Barth's comments about the present worth of the Scots Confession to see specifically how he relates to "tradition" in the form of a church confession.

Barth takes his cue from a famous passage in the Scots Confession itself which is surely one of the most significant utterances in Protestant church history. John Knox and his friends, while framing the original Confession, stated in the following terms the authority their confession was to have:

> Protesting that if any man will note in this our confession any article or sentence repugnant to God's Holy Word, that it would please him of his gentleness and for Christian charity's sake to admonish us of the same in writing; and we upon our honor and fidelity, by God's grace, do prom-

[17]*Credo* appeared in 1935 at the height of the struggle over Hitler within the German Church. *The Faith of the Church,* Meridian, New York, 1958, was a series of lectures given to French pastors in 1940-43. *Dogmatics in Outline* was given at the summer semester at Bonn in 1946.

[18]*The Heidelberg Catechism for Today,* John Knox Press, 1964.

[19]*The Knowledge of God and the Service of God,* Scribners, New York, 1939. These lectures, incidentally, represent the most remarkable theological *tour de force* of the century. The Gifford Lectures, according to Lord Gifford's will, must deal with natural theology. Barth does not believe in natural theology. Consequently, in his opening lecture he stated that believers in natural theology ought to be acquainted with the antithesis of their own position, and that he would therefore perform the function of describing for them that to which they were opposed. For the remaining 19½ lectures Barth made nary another reference to natural theology.

ise unto him satisfaction from the mouth of God, that is from his Holy Scriptures, or else reformation of that which he shall prove to be amiss.

The framers of the confession, Barth stresses, recognized its limited authority—it was to be followed only as it faithfully reflected the gospel found in Scripture. Wherever it could be demonstrated that it was *not* faithful to that same gospel, it was to be amended and reformed. To which Barth comments:

> That means manifestly that when we associate ourselves with this document, we must at the same time remain free in relation to it—free to give heed to the Scripture itself. The [Scots Confession] wishes to be read and understood as a signpost pointing to Scripture.[20]

Again, toward the end of his second series of lectures, stressing the human quality of this and other confessional statements, he writes:

> Such a decision or confession of faith, as the Scottish Confession, cannot under any conditions wish to usurp the place of the Word of God. It cannot claim a validity which is absolute and obligatory for all time. . . . It cannot bind men's consciences, it is not in principle free from error. It is and remains simply a human decision. . . . But within its own limits the Confession can be a human decision of such a kind, *that through it the way will not be blocked but rather opened up for the Word of God. . . .*[21]

So two things happen. First, we are liberated, and the opportunity is given to us, as Barth says, "to utter in weak, fallible, human words, humbly but joyfully, a confession of faith in the Word of God."[22] But secondly, the process of liberation gives us the opportunity and obligation of a *critical*

---

[20]*The Knowledge of God and the Service of God*, pp. 11-12.
[21]*Ibid.*, pp. 183-184, italics added.
[22]*Ibid.*, p. 155.

relation to the confession. The confession is not for us the last word, any more than it was for those who wrote it. As we read a confession, we must always ask ourselves whether it is or is not faithful to the gospel found in Scripture. And Barth at this point finds that confessions can sometimes help us to see the biblical faith more clearly—as, for example, at the point where both the Scots Confession and the Second Helvetic Confession rearticulate the doctrine of election in Christological terms. He also finds that occasionally we will discover that the confessions have not been faithful to the biblical witness. In dealing with the Scots Confession's treatment of Israel, for example, Barth finds himself dissatisfied. The statements, he says, "require at this point to be supplemented, or rather to be qualified, if they are to be completely intelligible. We must go farther than our Confession. There is something else which the Old Testament tells us about Israel. . . ."[23]

So the confession is, in Barth's words, "a signpost pointing to Scripture." It must never be confused with Scripture, but by making use of it, our own understanding of Scripture can be enhanced.

Barth himself has had a hand in writing what may turn out to be an enduring "church confession." In 1934, at the Synod of Barmen, it became clear that the Confessing Church had to speak a definitive and decisive word against Hitler. And this was done by the members of the Synod in the so-called "Barmen Declaration," for the writing of which Barth was largely responsible. The confession is solidly based on Scripture. And in confining itself almost entirely to theological statements, it turns out to be one of the most politically relevant documents the church has ever issued. It concentrates on the issue of Lordship. If Jesus Christ is Lord, as Scripture proclaims him to be, then we can give allegiance

---

[23]*Ibid.*, p. 62.

to no other Lord, no matter how pretentious or impressive his claims may be. Consequently, the first proposition reads:

> Jesus Christ, as He is attested to us in Holy Scripture, is the one Word of God, whom we have to hear and whom we have to trust and obey in life and in death.
>
> We condemn the false doctrine that the Church can and must recognize as God's revelation other events and powers, forms and truths apart from and alongside this One Word of God.

In other words, since Scripture tells us that Christ is Lord, Hitler cannot be Lord. Other "events and powers," such as Hitler, Nazism or anti-Semitism, must be repudiated.

IV. *Summary Statement*

After these two extended examples of the relation of Scripture to tradition, let us now draw together more formally some of the things implicit and explicit in Barth's approach. Three things may be suggested by way of summary.

1. The *church fathers* must always be listened to with respect, but we must be careful not to give them a veneration that leads to idolatry. Barth describes a visit to Wittenberg, where he saw inscribed on a stove, "The Word of God and the teaching of Luther will never fail!" But if there is always a danger of that kind of idolatry of the past, there is also the danger of prematurely jettisoning what can be learned from the past. "We are not," Barth says, "to play truant from the school of Luther and Calvin until we are better instructed, but to learn in [that school] what there is to be learned."[24] This can never mean simply using their words, no matter how appropriate the words may have been in their own day. Barth makes the point in words that deserve quotation *in extenso:*

---

[24]*Church Dogmatics,* I/2, p. 612.

There can be as little question of a repristination of the teaching of Luther and Calvin as of the orthodoxy of the seventeenth century in the present rediscovery and reacknowledgement of the authority of the Reformers. If there were, we would not be giving them the honor due to them, but refusing it. *Not those who repeat the doctrine most faithfully, but those who reflect upon it most faithfully so that they can then expound it as their own doctrine, are their most faithful pupils.*

But to reflect on their doctrine means to draw out the line indicated by them as it needs to be drawn in accordance with a new investigation of Scripture and the confession in reply to modern questions. As witnesses accredited by the confession of the Church of their day, they have ecclesiastical authority for the Church of today. Therefore the Church of today, with all the experience which it has since acquired, and the responsibility in which it itself stands, has to listen to them. This may mean deviation and contradiction as regards the historical form of their doctrine. The Church of today would not be accepting them if it were simply accepting or reproducing them in their historical form. It would be accepting them not as the Church of today, not as obedience to its own calling along the lines of the Reformation, but as an institute of antiquities—the worst dishonor of which it could be guilty for all its well-meant veneration.[25]

So tradition is not to be venerated for its own sake, and we are not called upon to repeat in our day exactly what the fathers said in theirs. However, we must listen to what the fathers said in their day, so that they can help to point us toward that to which they were pointing, namely the nature of biblical faith.

2. When we confront the past, we do not merely find the church fathers, we also find *the church confessions,* and the cumulative voice of the confessions speaks with greater effect

---

[25]*Ibid.,* p. 619, italics added.

than any individual theologian can do. Barth defines the conditions of a proper confession:

> A Church confession is a formulation and proclamation of the insight which the Church has been given in certain directions into the revelation attested by Scripture, reached on the basis of common deliberation and decision.[26]

This means that a confession will be a kind of commentary on Scripture, "in the speech of its age." It cannot be anything more than a commentary; it must not try to stand on the same level as Scripture. It thus clearly has limits: it is limited by its origin and by its object. It has geographical and temporal limits, which is why new confessions will always be needed, in order to confess the faith afresh in a new situation. As Barth's translators rather ungramatically render him, "In every case a new confession was needed which could not be a new one but only a new and preciser version of the old."

What then is the authority of a confession? The confession is authoritative as "a first commentary on Holy Scripture."[27] It is this as well as "a human word ranked before all other human words." Since nobody hears Scripture "purely," we have to test our hearing of Scripture against the confessions, but we also have to test our hearing of the confessions against Scripture. Since the Confession is "a signpost to Scripture," this means that a confession "becomes a constant antithesis, the horizon of our own thinking and speaking."[28] The confession confronts us with Christian history, it makes it necessary that we take into account what our forefathers have done and thought, it becomes a basis in terms of which we test our faith, and if we disagree with the confession, the burden of proof is always first of all upon us. We cannot

---

[26]*Ibid.*, p. 620.
[27]*Ibid.*, p. 649.
[28]*Ibid.*, p. 651.

"have done with the confession"; it is there to be reckoned with, even if we cannot fully accept it. If we go beyond such evaluations of a confession, Barth feels, we run the constant danger of equating revelation and church.

3. So the authority of the confession—and now of all "tradition"—can only be *a relative authority*. "What we know as dogma," Barth states, "is in principle fallible and therefore neither final nor unalterable." In the church confessions, he concludes,

> There can never be a final word, but only a word which is imperative and binding and authoritative until it is succeeded by something else. The Church confesses, and it also appropriates earlier and other confessions. But even as it does so, it remains open to the possibility that it may be better instructed by the Word of God, that it may know it better and therefore confess it better.[29]

Thus, when it comes to the place where each of us is called upon to make his own confession, to declare how it stands with him, to witness to the faith he holds, the individual is not left simply on his own resources:

> Before I myself make a confession I must myself have heard the confession of the Church, i.e. the confession of the rest of the church. . . . I cannot thrust myself into the debate about a right faith which goes on in the Church without first having listened. . . . If I have not heard the Church, I cannot speak to it. . . . And for that very reason I recognize an authority, a superiority in the Church; namely that the confession of others who were before me in the Church and are beside me in the Church is superior to my confession if this really is an accounting and responding in relation to my hearing and receiving of the Word of God, if it really is my confession as that of a member of the body of Christ.[30]

[29]*Ibid.*, p. 657.
[30]*Ibid.*, p. 589.

V. *Conclusion*

In the difficult area of the relationship of Scripture and tradition, Barth has broken some fresh ground upon which new approaches can be constructed. He delivers us from what can be a very perverse notion of *sola Scriptura* that would assert that we go to the Bible and to the Bible alone, as though in the process we could really bypass tradition. He delivers us from a kind of Biblicism that is content to rest simply with a parroting of the vindication, "the Bible says . . . , the Bible says. . . ." He confronts us with the necessity of taking tradition with utmost seriousness, and seeing it as a resource for the articulation of our own faith, so long as we keep it under Scripture and not alongside Scripture. He builds fences against the kind of subjectivism that is the morass of Protestant individualism, by pointing out that just as the church must first listen before it speaks, so must we first listen before we speak, and that when we do speak we may not jauntily set up our own private insights as though they had some kind of definitive worth simply because they are our insights. And he provides the supreme criterion by which all else, whether Scripture, tradition, church fathers, private insight, church structure, or whatever, must be judged —namely the criterion of the Lordship of Jesus Christ.

Whatever witnesses to the Lordship of Jesus Christ we must retain. Whatever jeopardizes the Lordship of Jesus Christ we must discard. That the issue between what to retain and what to discard is so momentous, constitutes both the glory and the risk of being a Christian.

THE MEANING OF TRADITION

by

John Meyendorff

The apostolic *kerygma* proclaimed to the world a historic event which happened "under Pontius Pilate," at a determined date and in a definite setting. This unique event was, on the one hand, the fulfillment of the whole history of the Old Testament—Jesus Christ is "he of whom it was spoken in the law and the prophets" (John 1:45)—and, on the other hand, it was the unique origin of universal salvation for succeeding generations. The essential meaning of the New Testament supposes that Christ's redemptive act has been completed once and for all, that nothing can be added to it and that there is no other way of benefiting from it but by hearing the Word of God proclaimed by the "witness." The Church is called "apostolic" by reference to these witnesses, and this adjective is even used in the Creed in order to make plain that the doctrine of the Church is in no way different from that of Christ's immediate disciples.

These fundamental principles must necessarily determine our attitude towards "Scripture" and "Tradition."

1. Scripture, Tradition, and the Church

Anyone familiar with Byzantine liturgical ethos, or with any other traditional rites, whether Western or Eastern, knows of the open and solemn *veneration of the Bible* which those rites require.[1] This veneration means more than the solemn reading of biblical passages, the constant repetition of verses from the Psalms, and the daily singing of hymns taken from the Old and New Testaments; it obviously means the

---

[1] Cf. our essay on "Bible and Tradition in the Orthodox Church" in *The Student World* (Geneva: 1958, No. 1), pp. 39-45.

43

veneration of Holy Scripture, in particular the Gospel, as a book: this is the meaning of the incensing and kissing of the Gospel, of the processions in which the Holy Book has the place of honor and represents Christ himself revealed in his Word.

The only possible purpose of this liturgical veneration of Scripture is to suggest to the faithful that it contains the very Truth of Revelation, which the Church possesses precisely in a given, written form. It is important to note, in this connection, that whatever value is attributed to Tradition and to the notion of the Church's continuity in the Truth and infallibility, the Christian Church never added its own doctrinal definitions to Scripture. Founded upon the Apostolic *kerygma,* it included, alongside the inspired literature of the Jews, the written evidence only of those who had seen the risen Lord with their own eyes and who could write down for the Church the very words of the Master, faithfully interpreting his teaching. The Church had only to define the "canon," not to compose inspired writings, because it never believed in any "continuous revelation," but only in the unique historical act of God, accomplished once and for all in Christ. The writings owed their authority to the fact that they had been composed by the ocular witnesses of Christ. The Church could only confirm this authenticity through the guidance of the Spirit promised by Jesus himself, not create it. This authenticity, of course, is to be understood in a very wide sense and as concerning certainly the content, but not necessarily the form of Scriptural texts: the Gospels of Mark and Luke, for instance, were considered as part of the canon from the very beginning, although they were not composed by members of the college of the Twelve, but the content of their *kerygma* was traditionally attributed to the evidence of Peter and Paul; similarly, early Christians, like Origen, who doubted the Pauline authenticity of *Hebrews* did not mean that it should be rejected from the canon, for they did not

44

doubt the fact that it was covered by Pauline authority in a wider sense than direct authorship. No one ever suggested, on the other hand, that anything besides apostolic writings should be included in the canon, and it is this general principle which determined the rejection of the *Shepherd of Hermas* and the *Epistle of Barnabas* from the canon of Scripture.

Apostolicity thus remained the basic criterion in the history of the formation of the canon, because it was also the only true characteristic of the Christian *kerygma* as such. The Church's intervention and judgment concerned only the *limits* of true Revelation, and in order to exercise this judgment it needed a criterion external to, but not independent from, Scripture. This criterion is the guidance of the Spirit, through which the Incarnation was realized and which abideth both upon Christ himself, and upon his Body, the Church. The Church, being the community of those who have received the salvation brought by concrete historical events, can have no other foundation than "the apostles and the prophets" (Eph. 2:20) who witnessed to "that which they have heard, which they have seen with their eyes, which their hands have touched" (I John 1:1), but this salvation of which they are witnesses has precisely this result of bringing God to live among us and of making the Spirit "guide us into all Truth" (John 16:3).

We have just said that Scripture contained the entirety of the apostolic witness. This entirety, however, is not a verbal entirety, just as the authenticity of Scriptural texts is not necessarily a formal or verbal authenticity. The Word of Life is not a theological encyclopedia which has only to be opened at the right page for the desired information to be found, exhaustively treated. Modern exegesis discovers more and more—as for instance the works of Oscar Cullmann, or Joachim Jeremias, have shown—that essential Christian truths, such as the doctrine of the Sacraments, not treated directly by the inspired authors, are considered by them as self-evident. Jesus' *logia* on the Bread of Heaven, the Vine, or "water springing up unto eternal life"—even if the sacramental interpretation of these passages is not the only possible one—cannot be fully understood if one ignores the fact that Christians in the first century practiced Baptism and performed the Eucharist. This makes it quite clear that Scripture, while complete in itself, presupposes Tradition, not as an addition, but as a *milieu* in which it becomes understandable and meaningful. At a time when no discussions occurred yet on the "number of sources" of Revelation, St. Basil of Cesarea, in a plain and almost naïve language, states the interdependence and essential unity of Scripture and Tradition in a famous passage of his *Treatise on the Holy Spirit*: "Among the doctrines and teachings preserved by the Church, we hold some from written sources, and we have collected others transmitted in an unexplicit form[2] from apostolic tradition. They have all the same value. . . . For if we were to try to put aside the unwritten customs as having as great force, we should, unknown to ourselves, be weakening the Gospel in its very essential; furthermore, we should be transforming the *kerygma* into mere word."[3] And he continues by referring explicitly to the rites of Christian initiation and the Eucharist.

There cannot be, therefore, any question about "two sources" of Revelation, and Revelation, in fact, is not a formal dictation of certain formally definable truths to the human mind: Revelation in Jesus-Christ is a new fellowship between God and man, established once and for all, a participation of man in divine life. Scripture does not create this participation: it witnesses, in a final and complete form, to the acts of God which realized it. In order to be fully under-

---

[2] Mystikos: this adverb, which can also mean "secretly" and "sacramentally," seems to be used here in order to imply that certain doctrines were kept in the closed Christian community, as opposed to Scriptures which were known to all.

[3] *De Spiritu Sancto,* 27.

stood, it requires the reality of the fellowship, which exists in the Church. Tradition is the sacramental continuity in history of the communion of Saints; in a way, it is the Church itself.

The Orthodox definitely believe in the absolute, organic, and infallible character of this continuity, and see it as implied by the very nature of Scripture. If this continuity was broken, Scripture would lose its meaning, and that which God wished to do through the Incarnation would in fact be a failure. Failures do, of course, occur in individual lives, in the lives of whole nations and societies, but the Church, as a gift of God, cannot be a failure, "for he wished to present it in splendor, without spot or wrinkle or any such thing, that she might be holy and without blemish" (Eph. 5: 27). The existence of this Church is a perfectly free gift of God, and its infallibility is in no sense deserved by those who compose it, but is solely the consequence of the fact that God indwells in her. All the members of the Church, every Christian community may succumb to sin as well as to error, but through that very fact they cut themselves off from the Church and must be reunited afresh through penitence.

2. *Tradition and Dogma*

While essentially and permanently self-identical, the Church lives in history. The divine Truth which abides in her must, therefore, always face new challenges and be expressed in new ways. The Christian message is not only to be kept unchangeable, but it must also be *understood* by those to whom it is sent by God; it must answer new questions posed by new generations. And here comes another function of holy Tradition: to make Scripture available and understandable to a changing and imperfect world in which neither problems and discussions nor simple references to Scripture are able by themselves to avoid error and heresy.

The history of doctrinal controversies, since the beginning of Christianity, shows the evident concern of major theologians and Fathers of the Church to preserve in their teaching not only the meaning of Scripture, but even its wording. This concern did not prevent them, however, from using non-scriptural terms when the defense of the Truth required it. In the fourth century, the Nicene Creed was carefully drawn so that only scriptural terms were originally used, and it is with the greatest difficulty that Athanasius of Alexandria succeeded in having the word homoousios included in order to express, in a language understandable in his time, a truth which Scripture presupposed. This example clearly illustrates the Church's awareness of possessing a living Truth which cannot be limited by purely biblical wording.

The verbal freedom which the Nicean fathers demonstrated was not, however, an internal liberty in the relation to the evidence of Scripture. The Orthodox Church has never proclaimed dogmas which are not direct interpretations of historical facts related in the Bible. Let us take a concrete and still relevant example, that of the veneration of Mary, the Mother of God. For the Orthodox, this veneration rests essentially on the dogma of the anti-Nestorian Council of Ephesus (431) which has in no way made any "Mariological" definition, but has simply condemned a doctrine, attributed to Nestorius, according to which Christ was a union of two "subjects": the Son of Mary and the Son of God. Since there was in Christ only one "subject"—the Son of God, who became also son of Mary—there is no one else of whom Mary could be the Mother, except the Son of God himself. She is, therefore, the "Mother of God," *Theotokos*. It is clear that the Council was essentially concerned with the understanding of an eminently biblical fact, the Incarnation: it is in order to express its full actuality that we recognize in Mary the "Mother of God" and not of a simple man, and consequently judge her worthy of quite exceptional veneration. On the

48

other hand, the doctrine of the Immaculate Conception appears to the Orthodox theologian as not only absent from the biblical narrative, but contrary to the biblical and traditional doctrine of the original sin. In the case of the Virgin's Assumption and bodily glorification, the tradition is formally preserved in Orthodox liturgical books and is very widely found in the patristic writings of the Byzantine Middle Ages. However, a definite uneasiness prevailed among the Orthodox with the proclamation of the dogma by Pius XII: the several, partly diverging, traditions which exist concerning the Assumption seem to them as belonging to a category of religious facts which essentially differs from those subject to doctrinal definitions. Scripture itself records similar cases— that of Elijah, for instance—whereas the absence of any reference to the death and glorification of the Virgin in the Bible seems to indicate clearly that these events played no essential part in the work of salvation as such, and that consequently there was no need for the Word of God to recount them and guarantee their authenticity. The entire Gospel changes in meaning if Christ is not one but two distinct subjects, while it remains strictly the same whether the Virgin was, or was not, glorified in her very body after her death. . . . This reserve, expressed almost unanimously by the Orthodox when the dogma of the Assumption was proclaimed, does not presuppose any *denial* of the corporal glorification of the Virgin, which is indeed testified by a fairly ancient tradition, for it certainly appears to be in conformity with the divine plan concerning which God "hath done great things" (Luke I :49). But no *theological* necessity seems to justify its inclusion among facts which realized the salvation of mankind.

These examples were brought forth here not for the sake of polemics on the issues which they involve, but in order to illustrate the Orthodox approach to the problem of "doctrinal development," whose meaning consists neither in a sort of continuous revelation, nor in making addition to Scripture, but in solving concrete problems in the name of an eternal Truth, the latter remaining essentially the same before and after the definition. This attitude is clearly reflected in the decisions of the early Councils. Here is the beginning of the Chalcedonian definition (451): "The wise and salutary formula of divine grace[4] *sufficed* for the perfect knowledge and confirmation of religion. . . . But, for as much as persons undertaking to make void the preaching of the truth have through their individual heresies given rise to empty babblings . . . , this present holy, great and ecumenical synod, desiring to exclude every device against the truth, and teaching that which is unchanged from the beginning, has decreed. . . ."[5]

The doctrinal definitions, which are normally made by Ecumenical Councils—but sometimes also by local councils, or through a simple general *consensus* of the Church—are final and irreformable inasmuch as they express the absolute Truth of Christ, living in his Church. As we have seen earlier, Tradition is but an expression of the permanent presence of God in the community of the New Israel. This presence is created by God himself, not by any external criterion or sign. Continuity, permanence and infallibility come from the fact that in every place and at every time there is "one Lord, one faith, one baptism" (Eph. 4: 4-5): no juridical criteria or conditions can replace this presence. This is why Church history knows many "pseudo-councils" (that of 449, for instance) which possessed the signs of ecumenicity, but were finally rejected, because they were not in the Truth, and also several councils which were not assembled as ecumenical, but later acquired an ecumenical authority. And, of course, the Orthodox Church, while acknowledging the moral authority of certain local churches, and, in particular, that of the

---

[4]The context shows that this "formula" is the Creed of Nicea-Constantinople.

[5]English text in *Nicene and Post-Nicene Fathers,* second series, vol. 14 (Grand Rapids, Michigan: Eerdmans), p. 203.

first among them, does not see any ecclesiological, or historical, reason to recognize in one particular episcopal see a final criterion of truth.

This lack, in Orthodox ecclesiology, of a clearly defined, precise, and permanent criterion of Truth besides God himself, Christ, and the Holy Spirit, is certainly one of the major contrasts between Orthodoxy and all classical Western ecclesiologies. In the West, the gradually developed theory of papal infallibility was opposed, after the collapse of the conciliar movement, by the Protestant affirmation of *Sola Scriptura*. The entire Western ecclesiological problem, since the sixteenth century, turned around this opposition of two *criteria,* two references of doctrinal *security,* while in Orthodoxy no need for, or necessity of, such a security was ever really felt, for the simple reason that the living Truth is its own criterion. This opposition was rightly emphasized, in the nineteenth century, by the Russian theologian A. S. Khomiakov, but it is based upon a concept of the Church which was already that of Irenaeus: "Where the Church is, there is the Spirit of God; and where the Spirit of God is, there is the Church, and every kind of grace; but the Spirit is Truth."[6]

3. Tradition and Traditions[7]

No clear notion of the true meaning of tradition can, however, be reached without constantly keeping in mind the well-known condemnation of "human traditions" by the Lord himself. The one Holy Tradition, which constitutes the self-identity of the Church through the ages and is the organic and visible expression of the life of the Spirit in the Church is not to be confused with the inevitable, often creative and

---

[6]*Adversus Haereses* III, 24, 1; English translation in *The Ante-Nicene Fathers* I (New York, 1925), p. 458.

[7]Cf. our essay, under this title, in *St. Vladimir's Seminary Quarterly,* vol. 6, no. 3 (1962), pp. 118-127.

positive, sometimes sinful and always relative accumulation of human traditions in the historical Church.

The distinction between "Tradition" and "traditions" is certainly one of the major tasks of the contemporary ecumenical dialogue, and it constitutes one of the most urgent responsibilities of Orthodox theologians. For even outside of its ecumenical involvement, the Orthodox church faces this problem with a particular acuity.

An Orthodox generally conceives his Christianity as an integral whole which finds its expression in doctrinal convictions as well as in liturgical worship and in whatever attitude he may take as a Christian. The psychological root of this attitude—quite different from that of an average Roman Catholic, who is much more ready to accept change when it comes from the proper authority—is the absence of an absolute, permanent doctrinal power, which we have noted in the preceding paragraph, and in the positive sense of *responsibility* that an Orthodox usually has for the *integrity* of his faith. He is, consciously or unconsciously, but rightly, aware of the fact that all acts of worship have some doctrinal implications and that true Christianity is to be taken as a whole set of beliefs and attitudes. At an elementary level, when he is not able to make the necessary distinctions between the essential and the secondary, he prefers to preserve *everything*. The formal and ritualistic conservatism of Eastern Christians undoubtedly played a positive role in history: it helped them to preserve their faith during the dark ages of the Mongolian and Turkish occupations. But it does not reflect as such the catholicity of the Church. Today, it represents a problem which Orthodox theologians have to handle if they want to face seriously not only the modern world and the Ecumenical Movement, but also, inside the Orthodox world itself, a number of reformist movements. And the first task of Orthodox theology today must be to rediscover, through a true sense of catholicity, the role of the one, holy

Tradition of the Church, as distinct from the pseudo absolute and human traditions. If one turns to the past of the Church, it is, in fact, surprising how many traditional authorities one can find to support this rediscovery, especially in documents related to the schism between East and West.

Since apostolic times, Christians have always conceived their unity as unity in faith, although it was obvious that every local church could express this faith in its own language, liturgical rite, and, originally, even in its own baptismal creed. This linguistic and liturgical variety did not at all prevent church unity from remaining a very practical reality. In the second century, Irenaeus could speak of a unique apostolic tradition equally well preserved in Rome, Smyrna, and Ephesus. When Christological controversies broke the unity of the Eastern Church, the situation began to change. The schism roughly followed existing cultural and linguistic boundaries, and a majority of non-Greek Eastern Christians—Copts, Syrians, Armenians, Ethiopians—adopted monophysitic confessions of faith. The Orthodox Chalcedonian churches followed Rome and Constantinople, and their influence was practically restricted to the Greco-Latin world of the late Roman Empire. Finally, this unity was itself broken with the great schism between the Ancient and the New Rome, again following racial and linguistic lines.

The prestige of these two centers was so great in their respective areas that all non-Roman and non-Constantinopolitan traditions tended to disappear during a long process of evolution lasting from the sixth to the twelfth century. Both sides started to recognize the ethos and practices of their respective metropolis as the only acceptable pattern. In the East, the ancient Egyptian, Syrian and Palestinian liturgies were gradually replaced, in the Orthodox Church, by the Byzantine rite. In the eleventh century, Patriarch Michael Cerularius, in his attacks against the Latins, was already firmly convinced that the practices accepted in the "city

53

guarded by God," i.e. Constantinople, constituted the only true Christian tradition: for him there was no longer any distinction between *the* Tradition of the Church and the local practices of the imperial capital.[8] His Latin opponents adopted an even sharper attitude in their famous decree of excommunication against Michael, deposed, on July 16, 1054, on the altar of St. Sophia.[9] The extreme point of the controversy was reached when Pope Innocent III, after the conquest of Constantinople by the Crusaders in 1204, thought for a moment that it was possible to realize an integrally Latin Christendom under his leadership.[10]

Fortunately, the Orthodox Church has always found in its midst a number of eminent witnesses faithful to the ancient catholic Tradition. The process of liturgical unification, according to the practice of the Great Church of Constantinople, did not prevent the translation of the Byzantine rite into the language of the various peoples converted to Orthodoxy. In fact, it was the use of the vernacular as the liturgical language that gave the Byzantine missionaries their principal element of success throughout the Middle Ages. It prevented the Greek Church from undergoing a fossilization comparable to that of the Nestorian and Monophysite churches in the Middle East.

On the other hand, the great Byzantine theologians were always conscious of the necessary distinction between "Tradition" and "traditions." In the very midst of the Greco-Latin disputes about rites and practices several voices were heard restoring the true scale of values, and it is good to keep their memory alive today.

---

[8]See especially his letter to Peter of Antioch, in Migne, P.G., 120, cc. 781-796.

[9]Text in Migne, P.L., 147, c. 1004.

[10]In his letters of that time, the Pope speaks of maintaining liturgy and practices in Constantinople in Greek only as a temporary tolerance (Migne, P.L., 216, c. 902; 215, c. 964 D-965 A); cf. O. Rousseau, "La question des rites entre Grecs et Latins des premiers siècles au concile de Florence" *Irénikon,* vol. XXII, no. 3, pp. 253-254; M. Jugie, *Le schisme byzantin* (Paris, 1941), p. 253.

Patriarch Photius is the first to be mentioned here. Condemned by Pope Nicholas I on the basis of canonical norms unknown in the East, Photius proclaimed the principle of coexistence, in the universal church, of all legitimate local traditions: "Everybody must preserve what was defined by common ecumenical decisions," he writes to Nicholas, "but a particular opinion of a church father, or a definition issued by a local council, can be followed by some and ignored by others. Thus, some people customarily shave their beards, others reject this practice through (local) conciliar decrees. Thus, as far as we are concerned, we consider it reprehensible to fast on Saturdays, except once a year (on Holy Saturday), while others fast on other Saturdays as well. Thus Tradition avoids disputes by making practice prevail over the rule. In Rome, there are no priests legitimately married, while our tradition permits men once married to be elevated to the priesthood. . . ." Photius alludes here to the legislation of the council *in Trullo,* or Quinisext (691), which Rome did not receive. He consciously avoids imposing it upon the Westerners, and finally establishes a general principle: "When the faith remains inviolate, the common and catholic decisions are also safe; a sensible man respects the practices and laws of others; he considers that it is neither wrong to observe them, nor illegal to violate them."[11] Faith alone, according to Photius, is thus the criterion for judging the practices of the local churches; nothing else can be opposed to their legitimate variety.[12]

Similar to that of Photius was the attitude of Peter, Patriarch of Antioch and correspondent of Michael Cerularius. He gave Michael the advice to restrict his criticism of the Latins

---

[11]Ep. 2, Migne, P.G., 102, cc. 604 D-605 D.

[12]In his encyclical of 867, Photius recurred to purely disciplinary and liturgical accusations against the Latins (Saturday fasting, sacerdotal celibacy, chrismation administered by bishops alone), but he had in view the Latin missionary activity in Bulgaria, an area which he considered as part of his Patriarchate and where Latin clergy were denying the validity of Greek practices. There is therefore no essential contradiction between his attitude in 861 and 867.

to the doctrinal question of the *filioque* and to consider the other standing points of litigation as "indifferent."[13] A contemporary, Theophylaetus, Greek archbishop of Ohrid, in a treatise consecrated to Greco-Latin polemics, also considers the question of the procession of the Holy Spirit as the only serious problem between Constantinople and Rome. Setting aside the liturgical and canonical accusations of Cerularius, he returns to the principle defined by Photius: "Unless one ignores ecclesiastical history, one will not use such arguments; only those practices can threaten church unity which have a doctrinal implication."[14]

In the fourteenth and the fifteenth centuries, all contacts between Greeks and Latins implicitly presupposed—at least in Byzantine minds—that reunified Christendom would preserve a variety of local traditions. Nicholas Cabasilas, in speaking of the *epiclesis* of the Spirit at the Eucharist, recalls the Latin rite itself as an argument in favor of the Byzantine position:[15] there is no doubt that for him the Latin liturgical tradition possesses a catholic authenticity.

In modern times, this attitude has become practically universal. In 1895, for instance, the Ecumenical Patriarch Anthimos and his synod expressed it in their reply to the encyclical *Praeclara gratulationis* of Pope Leo XIII: the union of the churches can be realized through unity of faith, but this unity does not imply a unification of "the order of the holy services, hymns, liturgical vestments and other similar things which, even when they preserve their former variety, do not endanger the essence and unity of the faith."[16]

The establishment of a clear distinction between the holy "Tradition" as such, and the human traditions created by

---

[13]Migne, P.G., 120, cc. 812 A-813 A.
[14]*Ibid.*, 126, c. 245 B.
[15]*Explanation of the Divine Liturgy*, XXX; trans. by J. M. Hussey and McNulty (London: SPCK, 1960).
[16]I. N. Karmires, *Ta dogmatikà kai symbolika mnemeia tes orthodóxou katholikes ekklesías*, vol. II (Athens, 1953), p. 935.

history, is probably the most essential aspect of contemporary theology, especially when and if it wants to be ecumenical. The very reality of Tradition, a *living* and organic reality, manifesting the presence of the Spirit in the Church and, therefore, also its *unity,* cannot be fully understood unless it is clearly distinguished from everything which creates a normal *diversity* inside the one Church. To disengage Holy Tradition from human traditions which tend to monopolize it is in fact a necessary condition of its preservation, for once it becomes petrified into the forms of a particular culture, it not only excludes the others and betrays the catholicity of the Church, but it also identifies itself with a passing and relative reality and is in danger of disappearing with it.

There lies a very urgent problem for contemporary Orthodoxy, especially in connection with its ecumenical responsibility and involvement. There was a time when the "Christian East" as such stirred enthusiasm in ecumenical circles as a beautiful, exotic and mysterious tradition, attractive because it was "different." With the growth of mutual knowledge and information, this phase now belongs to the past, simply because the Ecumenical Movement has been taken seriously by its participants: while still appreciative of the possible contributions which could be made by local traditions to the catholic reality of the *Una Sancta,* they look forward to the *one Church* itself. The *union of all* is the fundamental aim of ecumenical activity and thought. The obvious Orthodox responsibility is to show *where* this union can become a reality and *how* it can be realized. The claim of the Orthodox Church to be already the *Una Sancta* must be substantiated in the empirical reality of its life, so that it may really appear also as the *Catholica.* This is precisely the goal of the internal Reformation which the Roman Church is seeking presently in order to substantiate her own similar claim.

But all these efforts will bring forth fruit only if they end upon an *encounter,* not only with each other, but also with the Lord in the Spirit of Truth. To be truly "ecumenical" is to be ready, at every moment, for this encounter, which will come on a day, and at an hour, when we least expect it.

THE MEANING OF SCRIPTURE

by

George Tavard

The question of the meaning of Scripture acquires varied undertones according to our point of departure. This may be that of a preacher, to whom Scripture provides starting points and vivid illustrations for sermons, or, at the other extreme, that of a semitic philologist, whose professional concern is to determine the exact sense of terms and their semantic evolution through Hebraic literature. Between these, theologians try to read Scripture in keeping with the truth of philology, the *Veritas Hebraica* of St. Jerome, yet with the desire to catch something of the preacher's interest: Scripture is a source-book of religious insights that should be grasped as a coherent whole in relation to which the theological problems of each successive age may be viewed. Obviously, these points of view are bound to affect our understanding of the meaning of Scripture, for they color our approach and guide our reading. We search Holy Writ for the specific kind of meaning that we expect.

The modern problem of the meaning of Scripture ought to be seen against the background of its past reading in the Church.

1. Patristic Exegesis

Patristic exegesis is now well known, thanks to the works, among others, of Jean Daniélou and Henri de Lubac. It was typological, largely founded on the New Testament treatment of the Old Testament. St. Paul, interpreting the Rock of the Exodus from which water flowed as Christ (I Cor. 10:4), explained the Old Covenant in the light of the New. The New gives the authentic meaning of the Old. Jesus is the truth of all the patriarchs, the prophets and the holy men of the Old Covenant. The Church, as the gathering of the saints, is the meaning of the CaHaL in the wilderness, of the Temple and of the more recent Synagogue. Melchisedech signifies Christ (Hebr. 7:15-28); Abraham typifies the man of faith in Christ (Rom. 4). The admirable chapter 11 of Hebrews links the Old and the New by faith: by faith in Christ, the men of the Old Testament, looking forward to the fulfillment of God's promises, already lived in the New. "Faith is the assurance of things hoped for, the conviction of things not seen" (Hebr. 11:1). Only in the light and knowledge of the New can the Old be interpreted. As St. Augustine said, "Whatever is in these Scriptures rings in Christ."[1]

The passage from the interpretation of the Old Testament to that of the New runs into a difficulty. The Old Testament found its fulfillment, and thus its explanation, in the New, whereas the only fulfillment to which the New looks forward is the second coming of Christ and the restoration of all things in God. Called in the Apocalypse (14:6) the "eternal Gospel,"[2] this provides the sense and meaning of the New Testament. Yet we are in no position to read this sense and meaning, since the "eternal Gospel" will be an eschatological revelation. It is the mistake of all millenarists to look in this world, in human history, for sufficient anticipations of the "eternal Gospel" to be able to interpret the New Testament as the New interpreted the Old. If the Church interprets the Scriptures, she cannot do this by comparing them with the ultimate fulfillment of the New Testament. On the one hand, the Church does not now fulfill the New Testament as Christ fulfilled the Old. On the other, the conviction was already manifested in the first accounts of the Canon of the New Testament that the New Testament is also, in a sense, "eter-

---

[1]"Quidquid illarum scripturarum est, Christum sonat" (*P.L.*, vol. 35, col. 1989).
[2]On the theme of the eternal Gospel, see H. deLubac: *Histoire et Esprit* (Paris, 1950), pp. 217-227.

nal." The *Decretum Damasi,* after listing the books of the
Old Testament, continues: "also, the order of the Scriptures
of the New and Eternal Testament. . . ."[3] Since the New
Testament is also eternal, it can neither be departed from nor
be superseded in this world. Resistance to Montanism was
based upon that conviction. The *Decretum Gelasianum* begins with the statement that "the Catholic Church has been
established by God's grace" on "the prophetic, the evangelical
and the apostolical Scriptures."[4] Since it is said further that
the "only foundation" is Jesus Christ, it follows that the
Scriptures are the places where we learn about Jesus Christ:
they are also the "foundation," though not another foundation than Christ. The other scriptures that the Church receives
—the decrees of Nicea, Constantinople, Ephesus and Chal-
cedon—do not serve as "foundation," but for the "edification,"
of the church. Thus no ecclesiastical writings can ever constitute another Gospel than the one already given as New and
Eternal. For this reason the seventh Ecumenical Council
(2nd of Nicea, 787) described the function of the priesthood
as "the explanation of the divine Scriptures,"[5] and approved
the sentence of Denys: "The essence of our hierarchy is the
God-given *logia.*"[6]

If the Scriptures, especially of the New Testament, constitute the foundation of the Church and the essence of the
priestly hierarchy, their interpretation and explanation belong precisely to the "edification" of the Church and must be
provided by this hierarchy. As noted above, the interpretation
of the Old Testament was first guided by its fulfillment in
the New, so that Patristic exegesis was essentially typological.
Christ was anticipated in the great Old Testament themes,
like the Covenant, Exodus, the Passover, the Flood, the Ark.
Typology was not one key among others; it was *the* key that

[3]D.-S., n. 180.
[4]D.-S., n. 350; 352.
[5]Canon X, in *Conciliorum Oecumenicorum Decreta,* p. 123.
[6]Canon II, p. 116.

opened the field of the Older Scriptures. To some extent, it could also be the key to the New Testament. For the New and Eternal Covenant was not only embodied in the canonical Scriptures; it was also realized in the mystery of the Holy Eucharist. The typology of the divine Presence in the Church provided a key to the New Testament. It is for the Church, Hermas was assured in his vision, that the whole world has been created.[7] In her the meaning of the whole creation lies. The Fathers' appeal to the Church's *paradosis* went precisely to the partial fulfillment of the Eternal Gospel in her. Tradition was the transmission of the faith (*pistis*), the *kerygma* concerning the Father, the Son of God, the Spirit. The "virtue of this *paradosis*," according to Irenaeus, builds the Church, making it "one house" in protecting the faith, "one heart and one soul" in believing it, "one mouth" in preaching and transmitting it.[8] In so far as the promises of God are now fulfilled in her, the Church contains the rule by which Scripture is to be interpreted. She is not herself the *regula fidei*, but she knows the rule of faith. The meaning of the baptismal Creeds lies in their being a summary of the manifestation of God to the Church in faith. The Church's *paradosis* is her fidelity to the continuous manifestation of God to her heart. "The Church," Irenaeus explained, "has received from the apostles and the other disciples the faith which is in God, the Father, Pantocrator . . . and in the Son of God, the one who was made flesh for our salvation, and in the Holy Pneuma. . . ."[9] This reception from the past and its subsequent transmission to the future—which represents the social dimension of Tradition—results from the intimate experience of trust and belief included in *pistis*, by which credal formulas acquired revelatory meaning. In other words, there is

[7]*The Shepherd,* vision II, ch. 4. See *The Apostolic Fathers,* ed. by L. Schopp (Washington, 1946), p. 240.
[8]*Adversus Haereses,* bk. I, ch. 10, n. 2. See *Ante-Nicene Fathers,* I (New York, 1905), p. 331.
[9]*Adversus Haereses,* bk. I, ch. 10, n. 1; *Ante-Nicene Fathers,* p. 331.

an analogy of the Church by which Christians experience in her the truth of what Scripture narrates. In her the seed is sown; the bread is multiplied; the Christ is born; the Virgin is hailed by the Archangel; the Body and Blood are broken and shed for many for the remission of sins. Of all the contents of Scripture one may say what Origen wrote of the fall of Jericho: "Each one of us must fulfill these things in himself."[10] For this reason Tertullian denies Gnostics the right to read Scripture: only in the continuity of the Church is such a reading meaningful; those who are not in the continuous stream from the Apostles cannot understand the Scriptures because they cannot fulfill them. Where the Scriptures find no fulfillment, they have no sense either.

Walking a tightrope between the Montanist belief in an age of the Spirit and the Jewish belief that all Revelation is in the Old Testament, the Fathers determined the time of the Church as one of partial fulfillment and of lingering expectation. There is no ambiguity about Scripture itself, which is the Word of God, but about Tradition, which preserves, transmits, interprets the Word without being It, which guarantees the meaning of what is inspired without itself being inspired. Such a guarantee does not depend on the sayings and the contents of Scripture, since it interprets these contents, but it comes from continuous orthodoxy, succession in the right doctrine. "Before me," Augustine objected to the Manicheans, "there was Ambrose, who was not a Manichean; before him, Hilary and Gregory; before them, Cyprian and others, whom it would be too long to list, who were not Manicheans. And yet they taught the Church what they had learnt in the Church."[11] Where orthodoxy is held, the interpretation of Scripture is safe, for each implies the other. In the context of the living Church, therefore, there may be great freedom in explaining a given passage. Commentators may

---

[10]*Hom. in Jos.,* VII, 1-2. Quoted in de Lubac, p. 145.
[11]*Contra Julianum Opus Imperfectum;* P.L. vol. 45, col. 1125.

diverge; and different explanations may be proposed by one author. Thus Gregory the Great explains the Book of Job in its historical, in its allegorical or typical, and in its moral sense, passing from the first to the second and the third by a progression in depth, according to his correspondent's desire: "that I not only draw the words of history into the meaning of allegory, but that I also prolong the meaning of allegory into moral application."[12] In this Gregory followed the constant practice of the Fathers since Origen. That this method had Philonian antecedents does not affect its value, which derives from the fundamental principle of interpreting Scripture in the light and under the guidance of the Church's faith (allegorical, typical sense) and of her life and sacraments (moral sense). That typical and moral explanations never enjoy the finality of the literal (historical) sense of a text is unavoidable: although the Church's faith and life are true and, in a sense, divine, they are not now at the stage of their ultimate fulfillment. Only eschatologically will the allegorical and the moral sense of the New Testament be as exactly knowable as the literal meaning. The transition period in which the Church lives between the first and the second advent of Christ does not permit finality as to the form and formulation of our reading of the Word, but it permits continuity in faithful reading. This requires the *paradosis* of the truth to be, together with a transmission, a development, a progression in understanding.

2. *Medieval Exegesis*

The Middle Ages did not depart substantially from the patristic approach to Scripture. As has been pointed out

---

[12]". . . ut non solum verba historiae per allegoriarum sensus excuterem, sed allegoriarum sensus protinus in exercitium moralitatis inclinarem . . ." (*Morales sur Job,* dedication n. 1, S. Chr., n. *32,* p. 115).

many times, medieval piety was essentially a *lectio divina,* the inspired reading of the Bible. Medieval theology was a *commentarium,* a reflection on the Bible, as a result of which Sacred Scripture, the inspired text, became "sacred doctrine," that is, Sacred Scripture itself as ruminated by the saints and doctors in the Church.

This method of reflection became more and more systematic. On the one hand, it initiated itself little by little to a scientific approach to the literal sense, with the help of grammar and rhetoric, and, later, of linguistics, philology and history. On the other hand, following lines that were already well marked by the Church Fathers, it divided the spiritual senses into three, allegorical, anagogical and tropological, according to the three theological virtues, faith, hope and love. By focusing interpretation on the theological virtues, medieval theology made one major point: the meaning of the Bible remained something to be discovered by the Church rather than by learned and incisive individual research. The faith, hope and love which open the gates of the threefold sense of Scripture should be adequate to the infinity of the author of Scripture, and therefore they infinitely transcend each interpreter. They are the faith, hope and love of the Christian community, of the entire People of God. Individual interpreters can only suggest and propose meanings which necessarily fall short of the full truth. One must agree, with the "disciple" in John Scot Eriugena's *De Divisione Naturae,* that "the interpretation of Sacred Scripture is infinite."[13] That no explanation can exhaust the meaning of Scripture is a recurrent theme of medieval authors.

3. *Scripture's Self-Interpretation*

One can imagine how revolutionary the Protestant idea that Scripture interprets itself and that it is clear even to the

---

[13]*De Divisione Naturae,* D.L., vol. 122, col. 560.

simple, was bound to appear in the sixteenth century. Even the most moderate Protestant documents exhibited a certain uneasiness concerning the interpretation of Scripture. Once they had discarded the Church as an infallible interpreter, they were at pains to find a suitable medium of interpretation. The second Helvetic Confession (1566) declares:

> We do not acknowledge that which they call the instinct of the Church of Rome for the true and natural interpretation of the Scriptures, which forsooth the defenders of the Romish Church do strive to force all men simply to receive; but we acknowledge only that interpretation of Scriptures for orthodox and genuine which, being taken from the Scriptures themselves (that is, from the spirit of that tongue in which they were written, they being also weighed according to the circumstances and expounded according to the proportion of places, either of like or of unlike, also or more and plainer), accords with the rule of faith and charity, and makes notably for God's glory and man's salvation.[14]

The positive standard of interpretation appears to be twofold: the literal sense, arrived at with all available scientific means, and harmony with the rule of faith and charity. It is difficult to see what the latter may be, if it is not already the doctrine of the Church. As to the first, it leaves so much to the capabilities of scholars and their knowledge of the original tongue, the historical circumstances, etc., that the real meaning of the text seems to remain beyond reach. The Confession continues: "In controversies of religion or matters of faith, we cannot admit any other judge than God himself, pronouncing by the Holy Scriptures what is true, what is false, what is to be followed, or what is to be avoided." This is an ideal. But it does not solve the question of knowing precisely what God says through the Scriptures.

---

[14]"The Second Helvetic Confession," ed. by John H. Leith, in *Creeds of the Churches* (New York, 1963), pp. 135-136.

Protestant theology, especially in its Lutheran context,[15] has tried to solve this by searching for "a canon within the Canon," for a rule, contained in Scripture, by which the Scriptures may be interpreted. Luther established the principle in his preface to the Epistles of St. James and St. Jude (1528) : "A text which does not teach Christ is not apostolical, even if it be from Peter or Paul. A text which preaches Christ is apostolical, even if it be from Judas, Pilate, Anna or Herod."[16] Applying this to the New Testament Luther doubted the value of some books in which he did not see that "Christ" was preached. To which the Confession of Faith of Zurich (1545) protested: "We know well that we, men, must adapt ourselves to Scripture, and not adapt Scripture to our feelings."[17] For it is the fault of "our feelings" if we do not perceive Christ in the Scriptures. The question of a canon within the Canon brings us back to the interpretation of Scripture : if it is by the contents of its books that we can recognize Scripture, we must presumably be able to understand Scripture and discern its identity in our reading of it.

4. *Restricting the Scope of Scripture*

When these views, which constituted the classical theology of the Fathers and the Schoolmen, are formulated today, they meet the objection that several Catholic dogmas are not clearly formulated in Scripture: the Immaculate Conception, the Assumption, even if they have remote biblical sources, can hardly be accounted for by reading the Bible only; their origin must therefore lie outside, in a "second source" of doctrine. The strength of this remark cannot be denied. It also corresponds to the widespread Protestant fear that the

---

[15]See Hans Küng's remarks on Bultmann and Käsemann in *The Council in Action* (New York, 1963), pp. 135-136.
[16]*Works of Martin Luther*, vol. 6 (Philadelphia, 1932), p. 478.
[17]Quoted by Karl Barth, *Dogmatique*, I/II (Geneva, 1955), p. 20.

current return of Catholic thought to a theology of the Word, which restores first place to Scripture, is largely fictitious, differing from other theological positions in words rather than in reality. Admittedly the Catholic claim that "all is in Scripture" must have a different meaning from the corresponding Protestant claim, if the former is compatible with belief in the biblical basis of the Immaculate Conception, and the latter is not. Thus the Catholic upholders of the "Scriptural principle" find themselves caught in a cross-fire: on one side, Protestants object that some Catholic dogmas are not visible in Scripture, and therefore should not be dogmas; on the other, some Catholics object that the same dogmas are not visible in Scripture, and therefore should be attributed to an extra-scriptural source, which does away with the principle that "all is in Scripture."

What question does this raise in the first place? Before we can tell what is and what is not in Scripture, before we can even determine how to find out what is in Scripture, we ought to arrive at a clear idea of what Scripture is supposed to do for us, and determine for what we should look in it.

The polemics of the Reformation centered the discussion on how much of the Christian faith can be proved by Scripture. Thus the Thirty-Nine Articles of the Church of England stated: "Holy Scripture contains all things necessary to salvation: so that whatsoever is not read therein nor may be proved thereby, is not to be required of any man, that it should be believed as an article of the faith or be thought requisite or necessary to salvation" (art. VI). Among Lutherans, the Formula of Concord (1577) clearly explained what "rule or norm" it intended to follow:

> We believe, teach and confess that the prophetical and apostolical writings of the Old and the New Testaments constitute the sole rule or norm according to which all dogmas and doctors must be appreciated and judged. . . . Holy Scripture alone is acknowledged to be the judge, the

68

norm and the rule, by which, as by a touchstone, all dogmas must be tested and judged to see if they are pious or
unpious, true or false.[18]

Other documents are only "witnesses showing to what extent
and where the doctrine of the Prophets and the Apostles have
been kept in its integrity after apostolic times." By placing
on Scripture alone the burden of proving the faith and its
objects or contents, the Reformers invited Catholics to reply
along similar lines. The obvious answer was that Scripture
alone proves nothing, for it is a dead book, paper and ink.
"The Gospel," Albert Pio wrote, "does not consist of words,
but of their sense."[19] As written text, Scripture says nothing
without a discerning reader. If faith has to be proved, the
burden of proof cannot lie upon Scripture, but upon who-
ever reads it. And anyone who reads Scripture approaches
it with a number of assumptions in the light of which he reads,
so that the value of his interpretation depends on his assumptions as much as on the text itself. The point of view of the
Reformers, who refused any proof other than scriptural,
pushed Catholic theology toward a concern for proving the
faith. Scripture came then to be treated as one of the many
loci from which points of faith may be proved, along with
the writings of the Fathers, the documents of Popes, Councils and Bishops, the speculations of theologians, the testimonies of the faithful. Thus Scripture became necessarily
partial, presenting acceptable proofs for only a part of the
Church's doctrine.

The error made by most Catholic polemicists in the sixteenth century and by many afterwards lay in accepting the
point of departure assigned to them by the Reformers. Once
this principle had been adopted, there was little difference
between the assertions that Scripture does prove all the faith,

---

[18]"Formula Concordiae," pars I, Epitome, in Müller-Kolde, *Die
symbolischen Bücher der evangelisch-lutherischen Kirche* (Gütersloh,
1912), pp. 517-518.
[19]See my *Holy Writ or Holy Church*, p. 161.

or, on the contrary, that it proves only a part of it. On the point of the probative function of Scripture, the Reformation and the Counter-Reformation fell into the same sin, of singularly restricting the scope of Scripture. Scripture was not given by God to be "judge of controversy." For when it is, alone or not alone, "judge of controversy," it becomes a tool in the hands of men for theological investigation and argumentation and thereby ceases to be the Word of God manifesting itself with the power of the Spirit. The solution of the dilemma lies in a return to patristic thought. An interpretation of Scripture which looks for proofs is determined by the doctrines it wants to prove. Interpretation becomes, in this case, an attempt to read doctrines into the text of the New Testament. That these doctrines may be Protestant or Catholic does not justify such a method of reading.

That this is a danger—really, *the* danger—of all scriptural reading is patent enough to have been perceived by many. Correctives have been looked for which might, one way or another, guarantee the objectivity of our reading. All of them aim at making sure that the sense arrived at is the sense of the Holy Spirit. Unfortunately, the tendency, shared equally by Catholics and by Protestants, has been to make sure of the sense of the Holy Spirit through a more scientific understanding of the letter of Scripture. We then fall back upon the horns of the dilemma already outlined: the scientific reading of a text may well determine the notional sense conveyed by its words, but it cannot approach the real sense. After science has done its necessary work, the letter still remains to be personally understood and assimilated as spirit.

5. *Return to Spiritual Sense of the Bible*

Among the Reformers, Calvin seems to have been the most aware of the importance of the spiritual sense of the Bible. For this reason he insisted on the necessity of having the interior testimony of the Holy Spirit in order to understand the Bible as Word of God: "Although God alone be sufficient witness of himself in his Word, nonetheless this Word will obtain no faith within the hearts of men unless it be sealed by the interior testimony of the Spirit."[20] Thus Calvin recalled the earlier Church's concern for the sense of the Spirit, for the spiritual rather than the literal sense of Scripture. Both Protestantism and Catholicism thus invite us to return to the standpoint of the Fathers and the medieval Church and to search for the spiritual meaning of the Bible.

This doctrine may be epitomized in the following points:

1. The Holy Scripture of the New Testament embodies the communication of the Gospel as done in the Church of apostolic times. It is therefore the basic medium by which the Word of God is preached. In it the voice of the Apostles still resounds. From it the Word of God speaks still today to and through the Church.[21]

2. Since it embodies the Word speaking to the Church, Holy Scripture does not consist in a dead letter but in a living spirit. It is always the Word who communicates the Gospel in the Spirit. Scripture is therefore not the Word of God unless it is grasped in the Spirit. Only the Holy Spirit can, in ultimate analysis, interpret Scripture. Scriptural reading is not a matter of scientific exegesis or of human tradition, but of prophetic power. Christ "is the principle of all Revelation in his advent into the soul, and the basis of all authority in His advent into the flesh."[22] That is to say, the Christ of authority, manifested in the Scriptures, cannot be perceived unless one follows the "revelation" of the interior Christ present to the soul.

3. The Church, in her totality, is the instrument of the Spirit for interpreting Scripture. That is to say, the commu-

---

[20]*L'Institution Chrétienne,* bk. I, ch. VII, n. 4.
[21]See my *Theology of the Word* (New York, 1963).
[22]Bonaventure, Sermon on "Christ, The Only Master" (*Opera Omnia,* Quaracchi, vol. V, p. 568 a-b, n. 2).

nication of the Gospel (which is the Tradition) at any period of the Church interprets Scripture for that period. Since the communication of the Gospel is the Gospel, it is always true; apparent differences in the Tradition of diverse periods must be understood in terms of a continuing, developing, enlarging stream of doctrine. This implies that the Spirit raises prophetic men in the Church, who are enlightened by him to discern the spiritual meaning of Scripture.

4. Because it is unveiled by the Spirit, the spiritual sense of the Bible escapes all methods and techniques. No hermeneutic can guarantee it. The Fathers' approach has been characterized as "typological" because it viewed the spiritual sense of Scripture in relation to its fulfillment and model in Jesus, the antitype of all biblical images. The Middle Ages read the Scriptures in the light of the three theological virtues, each of which finds substance and food in them. More recent biblical theology has expressed it as a *sensus plenior,* which may be understood as the literal sense in its non-literal and theological dimensions and implications. These are approximations and can be no more. The spiritual sense is bound to escape scientific determination, just as much as the Spirit does.

5. The Church provides the necessary framework of the spiritual sense, in as far as she is the abode of the Spirit, wherein the Scriptures come to partial fulfillment in anticipation of their eternal and total fulfillment at the second Advent. This final fulfillment depends on the Spirit in the Church, and we may be certain that God will not remain without witnesses; he will see to it that the faithful are always aware of a minimum of spiritual interpretation, under which the New Testament would cease to be received as Word of God, and would be reduced to the status of a mere historical document.

6. Accordingly, the question of how much of Revelation may be known with certainty through Scripture alone raises a false problem: it assumes that Scripture has a noetic pur-

pose as a source of knowledge, rather than a kerygmatic purpose as the proclamation of a Word from God.

7. In his prologue to the *Breviloquium,* St. Bonaventure related the three senses of Scripture to the three Divine Persons. As God is Three Persons in one nature, so Scripture has three spiritual senses in one literal sense.[23] Another analogy is valid: the letter of Scripture is to its meaning what the humanity of Christ is to His Spirit. His body both veils and reveals His divine reality. The letter both hides and conveys the spiritual meaning. In the light of this, the Trinitarian analogy permits a still deeper grasp of the mystery of Scripture. The letter has no meaning but in and for the spirit, just as the Word is always known in the Spirit, and the Spirit must always be the Spirit of the Word. The Spirit comes from the Father through the Word, as the meaning comes from God through the letter.

I would therefore conclude that in order to make a solution of the problem of Scripture and Tradition possible, we should first accept squarely the standpoint that was universal until the end of the Middle Ages: Scripture is the Word of God, outside of which nothing has been revealed. If scientific exegesis cannot arrive at some of the Church's doctrines, we should remember that scientific study cannot by itself discern the sense of the Spirit. We should therefore continue this scientific study, with faith and in the light of the analogy of faith, until the Spirit, witnessing interiorly to the heart of the Church, graciously opens new insights into His mystery.

---

[23]*Breviloquium,* prologue, § 4, n. 2.

SOLA SCRIPTURA

by

Markus Barth

The formula *sola Scriptura* is a battle cry raised, as it seems, for the first time in the first half of the thirteenth century by Robert Grosseteste, and, within the next hundred and fifty years, by Roger Bacon and John Wyclif. It was originally meant to urge Christians to imitate Jesus Christ in his poverty, and it was directed against the riches of the secularized medieval church. Distinguished scholars like Marsilius of Padua, William of Ockham, Peter of Ailly and Gerson took it up in order to protest against the prevailing dominion of the Roman Curia. The Waldensians and Hus upheld it before it finally became a signet of the Reformation and its theology.

The words *sola Scriptura* are preferably to be interpreted not as a nominative but as an instrumental ablative, "by the Scripture alone." Thus the formula describes an efficient and normative instrument which God uses and puts into the hands of the church. The church, in turn, receives and uses the Bible as fountain and norm (*fons et norma*) of all true teaching on God, his revelation, his will, his actions. *Sola Scriptura* stands in Reformation theology beside *sola gratia* and *sola fide* (by grace alone, by faith alone). All these abbreviating formulae are dependent upon and directives to the perfect work and true proclamation of "Christ alone," *solus Christus*. Whenever a deification of the book, an identification of Bible and revelation, or a substitution of biblical words for the rule of the living God or the obedience of living men threatens to take place, the basic meaning of *sola Scriptura* is falsified. In the theology of the Reformers, both gratitude to God and discipline of thought, research, devotion and preaching are expressed by the confession that there is but one

75

Savior, one revelation, one salvation, one faith. The Bible is heard and proclaimed as the binding voice of the gracious judge; but the book itself is not made judge.

Since the beginning of the seventeenth century (Johann Gerhard) the caption *sola Scriptura* was called the *principium cognoscendi*. In 1826, A. Twesten, the successor of Schleiermacher, called it the "formal principle of the Reformation," and he elaborated upon its relation to Protestantism's "material principle," the doctrine of justification by faith. The introduction of the philosophical term "principle" and the distinction of a formal and material aspect of the Gospel and of faith bore seeds in themselves which had to lead, even within Protestantism, to the radical questioning of the formal authority of the Bible.

The Council of Trent, at its fourth session, in 1546, rejected a draft stating that the pure Gospel was contained *partim* in the Scriptures and *partim* in the oral tradition. But the Council pronounced that in questions of truth and discipline the same attitude of piety and the same reverence are due to Scripture and tradition. In the First Vatican Council this anti-Reformation declaration was reaffirmed. It tends to rebut or moderate the call *sola Scriptura* in unambiguous terms; but its positive content is vague and ambivalent. To the first session of the Second Vatican Council, in the fall of 1962, a Schema "On the Sources of Revelation" was submitted; its adoption would have broadened the gulf between Rome and all those confessing *sola Scriptura*. The Schema was not adopted but sent back to committee in order to be redrafted under the new title "On Revelation," which no longer excludes an *aggiornamento* in the direction of Reformation teaching. Oral tradition flowing from Rome maintains that the new draft will not come up for discussion and adoption during Vatican II. Even though this may be true, it cannot be denied that a substantial group of Roman Catholics is no longer willing to continue on the line officially taken at Trent.

Sola Scriptura

These are sketchy outlines of the historical situation from which any new discussion of *sola Scriptura* has to start, especially in an ecumenical working group like this. We observe that there have been Catholics before Trent, and that there are vocal Catholics, not to speak of Fathers and decrees of the Early Church, who support the grateful confession and necessary discipline which for a long time has appeared to be a peculiarity of Protestant Christianity. Catholics willing to learn and to confess *sola Scriptura* do not introduce novelty or heresy into the walls of Rome; but they enjoy and point out a light that was brightly shining despite some attempts (like those of Bellarmine) to put it under the bushel of church management. The purpose of the following is to invite both Protestants and Catholics together to rethink the issue thoroughly. A way should be found which avoids both a boastful attitude of Protestants—as though Catholics had finally seen the light we Protestants have always possessed and guarded—and a falling of Catholics into the same temptations which have led Protestants asunder and astray despite their fine "formal principle." Four images stand before my eye which may illustrate the necessity of such encouragement and warning:

a) The often-copied Luther statue showing a rather weighty Reformer pounding his Bible and defying all potential or actual criticism is a problematic exposition piece of the "spirit of Protestantism." If lawyers (at least in movies) adopt so pretentious a pose, it ought yet not to be copied by Christian theologians. Certainly the humanistic principle, *ad fontes,* back to the original sources, which is followed by the Reformers as by all conscientious scholars, is a fine thing; but it does not guarantee that the truth is spoken in love. It takes more than quotations rattled off in their original language to be a witness to truth.

b) In Protestant churches a visitor or worshipper may on occasion find an open Bible upon the altar, protected from dust by cellophane paper. The Bible thus exposed to the eyes and meditation of the worshipper, at the very place where a crucifix or tabernacle may be found in Catholic churches, cannot outbalance the damage done by an unbiblical sermon delivered from the pulpit nearby. If the Bible has become a symbol and is no longer a tool of actual living proclamation of Jesus Christ, either bibliolatry or neglect of the Bible begin to flourish under the very banner, *sola Scriptura.*

c) In Rome and Louvain, in Paris and Munich and in many other places, innumerable Catholic scholars are busily engaged in a new study of the biblical books. In recent years the number of Catholic biblical commentaries and monographs that I would consider first class is at least as great, if not greater than that of Protestant works. The danger of accepting dictation of Protestant questions, theories, and viewpoints that have proved strange or inadequate to the subject matters studied, is not always avoided by our Catholic colleagues; still, many among them are careful to learn from mistakes made in Protestant quarters and to push ahead in new directions.

d) A number of recent Catholic historical and dogmatical studies, among them those written by Y. Congar, K. Rahner and G. Tavard (and, perhaps the new draft "On Revelation" prepared for Vatican II?) contain critical challenges to both Roman and Protestant traditional ways of thought. Though it seems to me that it is not yet found, a way is sought to affirm the priority of the voice of God heard in the Bible over the church. Under heavy fire is the notion that the teaching of the church or the bishop of Rome is as infallible and unchangeable as the Revelation of God, and as authoritative as the prophetic and apostolic witness given to the church. The meaning of tradition is newly scruitinized. The Word, i.e. Jesus Christ, which God himself "delivered" to the hands of men, and the deliverance of men to the saving Gospel (cf. Rom. 6:17; 1:16-17), is distinguished from the traditions that informed or misformed the current message and shape of the church. It is important to note that at the same time Catholic historical, dogmatic, and biblical works are appearing and liturgical reforms are being introduced, all of which show the same converging tendencies, i.e., to listen and to submit oneself more carefully and thoroughly to the biblical witness.

Other images or visions might be added to the four described. But we must turn to our main topic. The formula *sola Scriptura* will in the following be illuminated and confirmed in three steps:

A. The uniqueness of the Bible will be delineated;

B. A warning against dubious apologetics will be raised;

C. Some conclusions will be drawn.

A. *The Uniqueness of the Bible*

1. *The Bible treats of two entirely different partners and of the amazing covenant by which they are established as friends.* This book contains a record of both, the revelation of God to man and of man by God. The act of revelation is in both cases not just a cognitive procedure; it is an act of salvation. God reveals himself by creating, sustaining, redeeming man. Man learns about himself by hearing and experiencing that God is for him and does not let him go. The sum of the Bible is the communion of God and man which is ultimately consummated and triumphant in Jesus Christ, very God and very man, who is in person the vindication of God and the justification of man, the king of faith and peace. God's conversation with the people headed by Christ is described in exemplary narratives, promises, exhortations, confessions. Most remarkable is the ample room given in the Bible to the (sometimes wise, sometimes foolish) human response to God. Man is not pressed into a mold; he is declared and made free to respond to God. The Bible is a charter of liberty, for it describes God's love in which he freely cares for man, and it describes man's liberation and appointment to be a happy servant and child of God even within the confines of created space and passing time. While good post-Biblical theological books or novels may have similar contents, they make it evident that the knowledge of such a God and acceptance of such an image of man is dependent on the Bible. Recent research has made the point that the Bible as a whole is both a result and a source of traditions. The biblical tradition itself is distinguished from the many traditions created or perpetuated among men by its exclusive concentration upon the covenant of the free God with the free man.

2. *The Bible is a Jewish book.* It was written most likely from beginning to end by people of Jewish origin who were promised and convinced that what they had experienced would be immediately relevant and applicable ("typical") to all men. By treating of that God who elects specific men at specific places in specific moments to do specific deeds, the Bible hurts the feelings of all men, whether they be Jews or Gentiles. Man prefers to believe in a God who keeps a safe distance or may be identified with generalities of timeless character. But the Bible speaks of him who in history has concretely manifested himself and who made chosen men bodily eyewitnesses and agents of his deeds. In contradistinction to the canonical books of the great world religions, the authors of the Bible expose the unworthiness of God's chosen men most drastically. They make it unmistakably plain that only by grace God is the God of man, and that only by grace man is accepted into the communion and service of God. But God always introduces himself as inseparable from his chosen (e.g., as "God of Abraham"), and his deeds are never described as facts that can be distinguished from the interpretation given to and passed on by his prophets and apostles. God's history with man is through Israel; again, it is consummated in the coming of the Son of God born from the Jewish

80

virgin Mary. By showing that he does call and justify sinners such as the Israelites and early Christians, God proves that he does not disdain any sinner (see e.g., the Book of Jonah and 1 Tim. 1:15-16).

3. *The Bible is a book of manifold testimony.* The Holy Scripture is a library composed of congealed oral traditions and writings which come from more than 1500 years of history. Since it did not fall from heaven in perfect shape, it contains not only differences and tensions, but also contradictions in both matters small and big. It is impossible to derive from it a "system of teaching"; for it is not a book of definitions and propositions. Teaching or instructing, in the biblical sense of the word, is the act of directing to a goal; it is strictly the opposite of subsuming God and his deeds under a comprehensive scheme of analysis and synthesis. Now the Bible gives instruction in the form of testimonies. It contains the voices of many witnesses—some testifying in the name of God to man, some pleading in the name of Israel or humanity with God. These voices challenge the hearers to listen, to discern, to answer with discrimination. Many a covenant lawsuit and many trials of God's elect in the Old Testament, the trial of Jesus and public testimony of the apostles according to the New Testament, form the frame in which the witnesses make their appearance. The reader of the Bible may in passing and for a little while be compared to a jury, judge, or public in court: he has to use reason to make up his mind, to decide for the truth wherever he discovers it, and to take a stand for it. There is no cheaper way to the truth as revealed by God than by seeking the Word of God in the words of man. Without love of the neighbor whom God uses as a witness, there is no love of God and no presence of his Spirit. And there is no other way to reveal one's perception of truth than by discovering one's own place in the judgment of God over the world, or, as it is called today, by existential involvement. It belongs to the uniqueness of the

81

Bible that neither in doctrinal nor in moral issues does it give pat answers that would release man from responsibility. God does not dictate right belief and conduct through the Bible. But he converses with us as with children (Hebr. 12:5); he asks us, "Why do you not judge for yourselves what is right" (Luke 12:5), he makes us realize, "God's way of righting wrong is revealed in the Gospel" (Rom. 1:17). Like all the parables, many things in the Bible are open-ended. The reader cannot remain passive, he has to contemplate and to cooperate. God trusts man so much that he will have man's free response, not a reaction of puppets or an echo from a well. Therefore, it is not amazing that no two Bible interpreters completely agree in all their results. Each man will have his "canon within the canon," i.e., he will prefer certain witnesses, topics, accounts, reasonings to others. The Bible resents and resists streamlining and goose-stepping. It contains and provokes an ecumenical unity in diversity.

4: The Scripture is like the kingdom of God, not from this world, but *in this world and for this world*. The shocking concreteness in matters of history, cultus and private conduct; the frequent exposition of dirty linen and depravity even of heroes; the secularity of parables and of political, juridical, moral or psychological diction found alongside technical priestly or late apostolic language; the wailing and the anguished cry resounding from the depth of filth and despair, match elements of the so-called ethical "high-religion" of a prophetic or mystic type. The human elements reveal the realism of the Bible—a realism which is not surpassed by naturalistic or existentialist modern drama. Flesh and death are not too far from God to be reached. The term "incarnation of the eternal Word" (cf. John 1:14; Hebr. 2:14-15) sums up the universal range of the Bible. This book makes everyone wonder by hitting God's elect people harder than those that seem far from God. Denouncements of the sin of the world are crowned with blasts against the wickedness of

Israel and the Church. "The judgment begins with the household of God" (1 Pet. 4:17). The judgment to which God submits "religion" of all kind is sharper than that pronounced upon self-styled atheists. The justification of the "ungodly" (Rom. 4:5) is a surprise which transcends the horizon of all optimism. From the scope of condemnation, confusion, forgiveness and hope expressed in this book nothing worldly is excluded. The bodily resurrection of Jesus Christ narrated, and the resurrection of the flesh announced in this book give courage to embrace a most positive attitude toward the world. The Bible is so worldly that many doubt its "religious value." But precisely this is the work of the Holy Spirit which originates and unifies the contents of this book: He makes the field of dry bones rustle with life and hope. In sum, because of its concern for mortal man, the Bible is the lowest among the holy books of the world's high religions. "Just as Christ is the eternal Word of God hidden in humanity, and just as Christ is honored and treated in the world, so it happens to the written word of God, too. It is a worm and no book when you compare it to other books" (Luther, *WA* 48, 31 :5ff.).

5. The Bible has proved to be a *liberating book*. Because it does not force man into a scheme, under propositions, by the use of legalistic or mechanical means, it makes surprising, puzzling, exhilarating reading. Even more, by proclaiming that God, the creator and judge of all, loves freely and wills nothing but voluntary love, it absolves man from the quest to find in natural (be it physical or moral) law or natural revelation anything higher, safer, more trustworthy than in the nature and will and deeds of God. By leading to ever new reformations within Israel, the church, and also within the development of human culture, this book has proved able to attest and exemplify man's freedom from both secular and religious bondage. Inasmuch as the Bible contains elements of wisdom originating outside Israel and the church, it opens its reader's eyes to look for truth, righteousness, and justice

83

wherever it may be found; it encourages them to test it against the precedents set by God and the drive of his Spirit, and it enables us to thank God for every sign revealing that —while he elects special people for special service—he is yet Lord of all men and is able to employ even Gentiles for his ends.

6. The Bible has been *"received"* or recognized as Holy Scripture *by all Christians* though the contents of their canons vary. The Protestant Canon follows, in the Old Testament part, the Jewish Masoretic Bible and counts 66 canonical books; the Catholic canon, as derived from the Septuagint and established in Florence 1442 and Trent 1546, numbers 72 books. The early process of Canonization (i.e., the Fathers of the time between ca. 150 and 400 A.D.) did not presume that the church could make the Bible holy, neither did they wish to exclude or forbid inspiration to occur in post-apostolic generations. Rather, canonization is an act of recognition by which assembled church representatives stated the fact that a given number of books were used in divine worship and were recommended to the use of the present and future generations. The word canon originally means "measuring rod"; but in discussions concerning the Bible it meant catalogue or list, before it received the sense of legal norm. Whenever Christians, consciously or not, put other authorities above or beside the Bible, their departure from the one canon has proved devisive. The church has had good experiences with obedience to the Bible and bad ones in disobeying it. We might compare the authority of the Fathers who formed the present canon to the authority of father and mother whom we are to honor. While they remain subject to the higher authority of God, which in exceptional cases may require that we "forsake" or "hate" them, it is promised that obedience to them will lead to "long life in the land." There is a pragmatic, if not utilitarian, element in respecting the parents and the canon which should neither be shunned nor glorified.

7. The Bible has proved *sufficient* to give that information on God and man from which we can live. We have no standard by which to judge what else besides the biblical contents might be edifying for our knowledge and service of God. There is no sound reason to oust or despise even those parts of the canon that are seldom used in liturgy, for private edification, or for popular preaching and teaching. Rather, gratitude moves us to say that the present variety and breadth, but also the concentricity and unity of the canonical books has proved a splendid tool for prayer and preaching, for guidance and confession. It is a unique feature of the Bible that it combines looseness and strictness, openness and definiteness, transcendence and immanence in such a way that its readers can never find rest in pat answers or provisional decisions derived from it. Though they may clearly see and bemoan the distortion or neglect of specific Bible texts in the church or world, they cannot completely despair. For God has proved willing and able to use now this, now that part or feature of the Bible for ever new reformations of the church and challenges to the world.

What can we do against the fact, the history, the power of this book? Resist it, neglect it, streamline its rugged edges, appropriate it for our own end, submit it to the company of supposed equals? All this has been tried, is being attempted, and will be essayed again. It is the uniqueness of the Bible that beyond any other thing found on earth, and despite all misuse, this book has been able to make men wise in matters of salvation, and to be useful for instruction and guidance (2 Tim. 3:16). Certainly we might speculate that God might have used other instruments also. But we have no way of sure knowledge that he did, does or will reject this tool. If we are to cling to what we do know, we recognize gratefully the uniqueness of this charter of liberty.

Now I realize that this "pragmatical" way of describing the authority of the Bible appears is out of line with the high and deep arguments found in the literature promoting this book. We turn to a brief consideration of arguments which, I believe, ought indeed to be shunned like the plague.

B. *Questionable Apologetics*

1. On the basis of observations gathered by specialists in the *history of religions,* two things might be said in favor of the Bible. a) All high religions are book religions; associated with subtle mediation between God and man are usually not only priest and temple, but in conjunction with them also holy writings. If Christianity wishes to retain its place among the high, it must not question the linkage between its own value and fate and the Bible. b) Whenever something is known or whispered about the origin of script, it leads to the realm of magic: the writing down of a contract, a debt, a promise, a law appeals to a general and primitive yearning for certainty and validity. Therefore, if Christianity desires to retain its appeal to both the uneducated and the sophisticated, it must stick to what is written. In either case abandonment of the script would threaten the respect which goes with antiquity and continuity. —It is obvious that such arguments cannot be of normative value. If the truth confessed and the unity enjoyed by the Christians were resting on a book rather than upon the living God and his self-manifestation in Jesus Christ and the Spirit, they had no reason whatsoever to claim any difference from the Old Egyptian belief in the Book of the Dead, or the Islamic view of the pre-existence of the Koran. In his Seventh Epistle and toward the end of Phaedros, Plato aired powerful arguments against writing; the apostle Paul occasionally pointed to the deadliness of the written letter (Rom. 7:6; 2 Cor. 3:6); Luther made a series of wonderful statements about the oral character of the Gospel as opposed to a legal code. Obvious resentments against the "Scripture principle," as vocalized e.g. by K. Adam and A.

86

Sabatier, appear justified as long as orthodox Protestants argue the superiority of sheer writtenness, rather than the content of the Bible.

2. There is a *humanistic or philological* argument that the use of primary sources is to be preferred to possible and actual distortion of basic information as is found in secondary and tertiary treatises, or even more in uncontrollable rumors and feelings. This reasoning is sound as regards academical or equivalent research work, even in matters theological. But since the church is not an academy, it cannot tie up its proclamation and confession to a methodology that all too easily and often has led to a sort of slavery to dead letters and has missed the living spirit blowing and the sublime truth attested in a given text. The fact that two hundred years of literary and source criticism have contributed at least as much to obscuring as to illuminating the biblical message, reveals the ambivalence of this approach to the Bible. Even a thorough knowledge of, and highest respect for the original biblical languages and the best attainable Bible text do not guarantee a deep understanding of the Bible.

3. A *legalistic* sort of reasoning equates the Bible readily with a law. In the time of Jesus the party of the Sadducees accepted only the five books of Moses as canonical; they felt that this restriction of the canon was necessary to keep out the dangerous influence of strange elements to which all those were exposed who accepted prophetic books, wisdom style literature, and oral traditions. Augustine was convinced that just as scientific reasoning is dependent upon visible things, so faith had to rely upon supernatural authority. Like Tertullian he used the term *instrumentum* (in its legal meaning, which may approach our term evidence) as a fitting description of the Bible's function in the search for truth. The development of Canon Law before and after Gratian (12th century) may at best be interpreted as an attempt to preserve, and to give an unambiguous form to, the contents of God's

revelation as they were delivered to the Catholic Church in Scripture and oral tradition. Factually, however, under the hands of the legalist managers of revelation, the Bible and the dogmas have often become equated with primary legal materials. The Reformation concepts *regula et norma* still contain elements of a legalistic view and use of the Bible. Among recent Protestants, the Fundamentalist B. B. Warfield is bold enough simply to identify inspiration and prophecy with law. Indeed, Paul speaks of "the canon" valid in the "new creation" (Gal. 6:15-16) and of the law of Christ or of the Spirit (Gal. 6:2; Rom. 8:2); James refers to the "law of liberty" (1:25; 2:8,12); the concept "new commandment" is used in the Johannine literature. But the superceding of a period of law by the law's fulfillment through Jesus Christ, the fulfilled promise of the writing of the law into the hearts of men rather than upon tablets, and the glorious work ascribed to the Holy Spirit in the New Testament forbid the notion that in the hands of Christ and the Christians the Bible fulfills nothing else but the function of a constitution, law or statute. Rather the Bible becomes through Jesus Christ a charter of liberty which is validated through two events: first, the submission of Jesus to the law; and second, the ongoing operation of the Spirit in the community of God's people. Without the voluntary obedience of Jesus Christ and without the freedom granted to and shown by the children of God, the Bible is null and void, even as a law. No less a man than the apostle Paul, trained in God's law and full of respect to his Bible as he was, spoke of the "oldness" and killing character of the (biblical) letter.

4. *Philosophical* reasoning for the authority is, e.g., found wherever epistomology and soteriology, or a formal and material principle of faith, have been nicely distinguished. Indeed, as was stated much earlier, Protestants have boasted, probably under the influence of philosophical idealism, about possessing the right formal principle (i.e., *sola Scriptura*),

thereby complementing the material principle *sola gratia*. We observe that the possession of these principles was not strong enough to free them from the temptation of leaning heavily upon natural theology and natural law in their doctrinal and ethical teachings. Not until the theology of K. Barth were the full epistemological consequences drawn from the *sola gratia*. If we are saved only by the special grace given in Jesus Christ, then we also are enlightened only by the light of the same Jesus Christ. In the Bible itself revelation and salvation, or knowledge and eternal life, cannot be distinguished as sharply as methodology and ontology would have to be in philosophical thought. The Old Testament concept *dabar* comprehends both word and event; the New Testament concept Gospel is characterized as "power of salvation" (Rom. 1:16f.). "To know thee is eternal life" (John 17:3). While God has graciously given to man the Bible as a testimony to that revelation which is salvation, he has not given into the hands of man a methodology or principle which will automatically lead to truth and life. There is a German proverb, "The way to hell is paved with good principles." Indeed, church history is full not only of wonderful acts of witness and obedience, but also of atrocious deeds committed under the slogan, *sola Scriptura*.

5. On the *pragmatical* level it has been argued (especially in Roman Catholic quarters, in the heat of anti-Reformation fights) that the Bible has only as much authority as the church attributes to it, or negatively that the Bible would have no authority unless the church had given it. If this were true the supreme authority of the Bible would somehow be dependent upon the even more supreme authority of the church. However, the history of Israel and of the church show unmistakably that God's people is kept alive and renewed again and again not by its own self-regenerating power, but by the word of God spoken to it and heard afresh. Therefore, it is the self-authenticating power of the Spirit over the church and the

world, not the control of the church over the Spirit and its works, to which the authority of the Bible must be ascribed. Not only when the church obeys and submits to the Biblical witness, but even more when the biblical voices resound against a disobedient church, is the Bible's authority established.

6. We ascend to a higher level of discussing the authority of the Bible when we come to the *Christological* argument. Since the days of Origen, time and again it has been suggested that the uniqueness of the Bible exists in its dual nature. It was argued that this book is at the same time word of God and word of man; both are unmixedly and inseparably contained and expressed in it—just as Jesus Christ is very God and very man. For Origen the one incarnation of the Eternal Word was not simply over and done with with the birth, crucifixion and assumption of Jesus. But the one incorporation of the Word gave testimony to the eternal assumption of human flesh into communion with God: which finds at least a threefold (sacramental) expression in the time of the church: (1) by the union of the body of Christ with the Eucharistic host upon the altar; (2) by the union of Christ and his church expressed by the Pauline term "body of Christ"; and (3) by the union of eternal and human word in the Bible. Recent neo-Origenistic scholars of various denominational background have called these incorporations an "extension of the incarnation." Indeed, if the Bible were such a direct bodily extension of Jesus Christ, it would possess unique authority. But it would still have to share this authority with the mysteries of the Eucharist and of the Mystic Body of Christ, i.e., the Church. Some differences between Eastern Orthodox, Roman Catholic and Protestant Christians resemble a wrangle over which of those "extensions" is prior or superior to the others. No solution is in sight as long as nothing but claims meet with claims. Actually it is a most dubious enterprise to speak of an extension of the incarnation. For the incarnation

of the eternal Word includes the unique events of birth, crucifixion, and ascension of Jesus Christ; it is a miracle in history,
not a timeless principle. It is to be attested to and glorified,
because it is once and for all, *ephapax;* it is not to be repeated
or re-enacted like a myth. It is sufficient and ever present before God and man through the operation of the Spirit. The
assembly of the faithful, the celebration of the Lord's Supper,
the use of the Bible are most necessary and appropriate means
to worship the Father, the Son and the Spirit. But precisely
in worship no creature will equate itself or equate something
created with God. We conclude: The Bible is not to be called
the extended incarnation. Its authority derives from the authorization by God of the men whose testimony is heard from
its pages; it does not derive from a miracle of inscripturation
of the Spirit in a book which would be analogous to the incarnation of the Word.

7. In conclusion, it is unwise in any form whatsoever to
speak of the *"absolute authority* of the Bible." For the Bible
is in no wise an absolute. Its witness to truth, its power to call
to life, its teaching of wisdom is relative to the consummation
of the covenant between God and man, made in Jesus Christ.
And it is relative to the authorization of prophets and apostles
to be proclaimants of God before many and intercessories for
the many. Finally it is relative to the Holy Spirit. While the
first and second of these relationships are undisputed, the
third requires three additional comments.

It is necessary to speak of inspiration when the Bible's
authority is discussed—though the ways and means of inspiration defy any sort of rationalization or unambiguous
description; human authors are in different ways conscious
of and contributing to the heavenly and earthly things about
which they testify. But it is also necessary to state that, according to the Bible, inspiration is a manifestation and presence of God that happens to men, not to things (such as the

FORSYTH LIBRARY
FORT HAYS KANSAS STATE COLLEGE

staff of Moses, the temple on Zion, or book scrolls written by holy men).

Inspiration occurs to sinful men who are tested and tempted in the service of God and who fall into sin and have to be raised again by grace; Jesus Christ is the only one upon whom the Spirit "remains" (John 1:32-33), and who is tempted without falling into sin. Therefore, inspiration cannot be generally equated with the bestowal of inerrancy or infallibility. The theory that the biblical writers, because inspired, are also infallible tends to make them second Christs. It also presupposes that the readers of the Bible are in a position to pass judgment on the relationship between the Bible and truth, after comparing the two. No man should pretend to be in that position; therefore, no man should believe that he makes a sensible and meaningful statement when he affirms that in matters of fact and faith the Bible never errs, in matters of conduct and decisions it never fails. If he nevertheless does, he rather asserts his own than the Bible's authority.

The inspiration of chosen men of God is recognized only by inspired men. The same Spirit must operate there and here. Thanks to inspiration by God, Peter recognizes that Jesus is the Messiah (Matt. 16:16-17). Because the Corinthians are given the same Spirit which the apostle Paul received, they can discern the spiritual things communicated to them (1 Cor. 2:9-15). Unless the same Spirit gives understanding and life to those using the Bible, the Bible remains a book like others. Therefore, its authority is not absolute but always relative to God and faith in God.

C. Conclusions

The purpose of the seven critical points following upon the positive presentation of *sola Scriptura* was not to display or to encourage a general skepticism or relativism, but rather to warn both Protestants and Catholics: *Corruptio optimi pes-*

sima! Sola Scriptura may do harm as well as good. Idolatry and crimes are not automatically excluded by the endorsement of a fine directive. Protestants have sometimes made it difficult for Catholics to understand what *sola Scriptura* could mean. Whenever they gave the impression of men possessing a law and willing to subject everyone to their own absolute principle, they were hardly convincing witnesses for the freedom of God's children. While Catholics no longer boast that they have nothing to learn from their "separated brethren," Protestants are no less in need of repentance. If there is readiness on both sides not to discuss principles but simply to follow the directive *sola Scriptura,* then praise will be given to God and not to a body of fallible men.

What we need is not a stiffer doctrine of the Bible, but a greater enjoyment of the contents of the Bible and a better use of the Book. *Laudes Sacrae Scripturae,* praising God for the gift and usefulness of this book, rather than legal definitions or zealous enforcements is the way to confess our indebtedness. The Bible is not to be used as a sledge hammer to crush the freedom of man, of his search for truth, of various responses to God and to the challenges of life. It is rather a liberating documentation of different testimonies inspired by God and acceptable to him. Thus *sola Scriptura* is not by definition opposed to tradition; but it urges all men to distinguish between God's act of delivering himself into the hands of man which delivers us into his hands, and man-made traditions by which we all too often attempt to monopolize or captivate God and to exclude men from community with him. Also *sola Scriptura* is not directed against the church—as if a man with Bible in hand would have the right to feel superior to the church who delivered the book to him—but the directive is an invitation to ever new repentance of every Christian, and to a continuous reformation of the whole church through ever new obedience to God's revelation. To put it very bluntly: the Bible itself is neither the truth, nor the life, nor the way; for it is not a second Christ and it does not compete with the Lord who is the Spirit. But because of its relationship to the Spirit, it is for both bishop and every "man of God" a tool which has proved indispensable and does prove uniquely "useful" for the building of the church and for its witness to the world. *Tolle, lege,* 2 Tim. 3:14-17!

THE RELEVANCE OF OLD TESTAMENT STUDIES FOR ECUMENISM

by

Roland E. Murphy, O. Carm.

On November 24, 1962, Professor Oscar Cullmann delivered an address to representatives of the press in the name of the non-Catholic observers at Vatican Council II. In the course of his remarks he stated that "it is a fact that dialogue began among exegetes. Today it has spread to all theologians." The words of another observer at the Council, Professor Edmund Schlink of Heidelberg University, are even more explicit:

What are the factors which have contributed new impetus to the ecumenical dialogue? Here one must mention first the intense and fruitful encounter and cooperation between Evangelical and Catholic biblical scholarship. Ever since Catholic exegesis was freed from the narrowness of guarding against Modernism, by the biblical encyclical of Pope Pius XII, it has made considerable progress. This encyclical very emphatically set up as a goal the study of the historical sense of the Bible, the meaning which the author of the biblical text intended to convey. Hence Catholics employ the same methods and meet the same problems as their colleagues of the Evangelical Church. These problems are no longer covered over by later interpretations of the Church and by maneuvering with a multiplicity of biblical meanings. By means of a common use of historico-critical methods an astounding measure of agreement has been reached, even in the understanding of such texts which in previous centuries were much debated by Evangelical and Catholic theologians. This is true, in part, even for the understanding of the Pauline teaching on justification.[1]

---

[1] E. Schlink, "Themen des zweiten Vatikanischen Konzils in evangelischer Sicht," *Kerygma und Dogma* 9 (1963), p. 177.

The purpose of this paper is to spell out that dialogue in some detail. It may be said at once that the role of Old Testament studies has been modest, although important. It may justly be claimed that New Testament studies remain more important for the dialogue, for it is here that serious differences still exist. How does the Church relate to the New Testament? Is development in doctrine compatible with the biblical message? These questions point clearly to the New Testament as the sensitive area. Yet this can be explored in mutual respect and with mutual profit by both Catholics and non-Catholics in these days because of the rapprochement that seems to be most obvious in Old Testament studies.

1. *Historical Perspective*

The most important single factor that makes it even possible to speak of relevance is the encyclical of 1943, *Divino afflante Spiritu*.[2] This document marked the definitive acceptance of the historico-critical method in Catholic biblical exegesis.[3] I do not mean that this methodology was not practiced by Catholic scholars before this—one need only recall Père Lagrange[4]—but never before had there been such strong emphasis from the official source. The progress made in the scientific understanding of Old Testament literature, especially the Pentateuch, played a significant role in bringing about this recognition.

---

[2]For the text of the encyclical, cf. *Rome and the Study of Scripture* (St. Meinrad, Ind., 1962), pp. 80-107. There is a brief historical evaluation of the encyclical in *Chicago Studies 2* (1963), pp. 16-28, by the present writer, and the total historical context is well described by J. Levie, S.J., *The Bible, Word of God in Words of Men* (New York, 1961).
[3]This is recognized by G. Ebeling, even if he questions the ultimate relevance of the method within the Church; see his ambiguous appraisal in *Word and Faith* (Philadelphia, 1963), pp. 52-55.
[4]F. Braun, O.P., *The Work of Père Lagrange*, ed. R. T. A. Murphy (Milwaukee, 1963).

From the days of the Biblical Commission decrees[5] on Mosaic authorship of the Pentateuch (1906) and the historical character of Genesis 1-3 (1909), the Pentateuch had become the touchstone of critical methodology. It is not an exaggeration to say that all the progress in this area was achieved by the labors of Protestant scholars. Looking back, the historian can see that the very errors and extravagances of the documentary theory which is associated with the name of Julius Wellhausen were inevitable. There seemed to be no escape from the tight world of J,E,P,D, the documents written down so long after the Mosaic period. The striking fact is that the historico-critical methodology itself exposed the errors of the Wellhausen reconstruction.[6] Gradually the Catholic Church took a careful look at what could be called the more or less assured results of scholarly research. Thus, by 1948 there was a clear admission of development in the historical and legal narratives of the Pentateuch and a frank acknowledgement of the complex type of "history" to be found in Genesis 1-11.[7] This enlightened exegetical position was a recognition of the historicality of the Old Testament, of the milieu in which it was formed and handed down. More than in any other sector of biblical study, the break-through in the Pentateuchal question was fundamental for the general progress of Catholic Old Testament biblical studies.

---

[5]These decrees are available in the pamphlet cited above in note 1, *Rome and the Study of Scripture.*

[6]J. Coppens, *The Old Testament and the Critics* (Paterson, N.J., 1942), provides a brief sketch of the vagaries of Pentateuchal criticism; see also the valuable summary by C. R. North in *The Old Testament and Modern Study,* ed. H. H. Rowley (Oxford, 1951), pp. 48-83.

[7]Cf. the reply of the Biblical Commission to the questions of Cardinal Suhard in *Rome and the Study of Scripture,* pp. 150-153. A fundamental mistake in the earlier approach to the Pentateuchal question was the uncritical acceptance of biblical tradition as an answer to questions concerning literary authorship. The Biblical Commission itself seems to have recently provided a sharp distinction between merely literary matters and dogmatic truths; cf. E. Siegman, "The Decrees of the Pontifical Biblical Commission," *Catholic Biblical Quarterly* 18 (1956), pp. 23-29.

It was the archeological discovery of the ancient Near East which made possible the re-evaluation, not only of the composition of the Pentateuch, but of many other problems, such as the liturgical origins of Psalms and the whole problem of literary forms, the phenomenon of wisdom literature, the background of the creation stories, the nature of Old Testament history, etc. Both Catholic and non-Catholic scholars were engaged in the discovery and the application of the new data, from Ur to Ugarit, to the Old Testament. On this level of purely historical interpretation there emerged a large consensus of agreement in the community of scholars.

The interchange of ideas was almost completely restricted to Europe in the beginning. Here the situation was more favorable to give and take, especially in the German universities that housed both Catholic and Evangelical theological faculties. A realistic judgment of American Catholic participation can be gained by an examination of the *Catholic Biblical Quarterly;* the stance of the first thirteen volumes is in lively contrast to the openness and awareness that characterizes volumes XIII-XXVI.[8] Several factors have been at work to improve the American scene. There have been greater opportunities for training, such as in the Semitic department of the Catholic University of America, and at the Johns Hopkins University where Professor W. F. Albright has been the mentor of many Catholic as well as non-Catholic students. The growing contacts between American Catholic and non-Catholic scholars has led to a mutual exchange of representatives at the annual meetings of the Catholic Biblical Association and the Society of Biblical Literature. And both

---

[8]The Old Testament jubilee issue of the January, 1963, *CBQ* contained articles by two Protestants (W. Albright, G. Fohrer) and a Jewish scholar (E. Speiser). There has been mutual cooperation in writing for the biblical journals, Protestants contributing to *CBQ,* and Catholics contributing to the *JBL;* most noteworthy of the Catholic contributions to the latter is J. L. McKenzie, S.J., "Problems of Hermeneutics in Roman Catholic Exegesis," *Journal of Biblical Literature* 77 (1958), pp. 197-204.

organizations have appointed committees to explore further avenues of mutual interest.

The biblical movement has not failed to meet resistance, however, particularly in Rome where the Pontifical Biblical Institute was subjected to sharp attack.[9] This resistance is comparable to the unyielding fundamentalism familiar to Protestants from such quarters as *Christianity Today*. But not all of the reaction was of this type. Outstanding in its tone and constructive approach was the essay of Karl Rahner.[10] He acknowledges that the tensions within Catholic theology are more in the field of New Testament than Old Testament study, although about thirty years ago it was surprisingly just the opposite. He addresses exegetes and encourages them to look to the theological implications of their work and to their task of correlating biblical data with the doctrine of the Church. All would agree that a more effective *modus vivendi* between Scripture and dogmatic theology is one of the most urgent tasks facing Catholic scholars. To this end, the proper evaluation of Scripture as a theological tool or source must be reached.

2. *Areas of Exegetical Dialogue*

It is hardly pertinent here to exemplify the consensus of agreement between Catholic and non-Catholic exegetes in the remote areas of Semitic philology or other subsidiary biblical

---

[9]For a clear summary of developments, cf. J. A. Fitzmyer, S.J., "A Recent Roman Scriptural Controversy," *Theological Studies* 22 (1961), pp. 426-444. An impartial viewpoint expressed by a Greek Orthodox theologian, W. S. Schnierla, is to be found in *St. Vladimir's Quarterly Review*, Summer, 1962, reprinted in *Cross Currents* 12 (1962), pp. 407-421. The controversy was reflected in many other magazines, such as the *New Yorker* (Xavier Rynne) and *Time*. Echoes of the conflict in the United States can be seen in the stance taken by the *American Ecclesiastical Review*.

[10]"Exegese und Dogmatik," *Stimmen der Zeit* 168 (1960/61), pp. 241-262, which is very briefly reported in *Theology Digest* 10 (1962), pp. 84-86.

sciences. Agreement on this level is to be expected. We will consider some central issues of Old Testament interpretation which are at the same time most promising.

The role of tradition in the composition of the Old Testament is such an issue, and the sub-titles of Gerhard von Rad's *Theology of the Old Testament* can be instanced for the new direction of thought. His two volumes are entitled: I, *The Theology of Israel's Historical Traditions;* II, *The Theology of Israel's Prophetical Traditions.* It is safe to say that the word "tradition" was anathema to the majority of older Protestant scholars. The biblical witers, and especially the prophets, were considered to be creators, not tradents. They were supposedly religious geniuses, men of original and penetrating insight into the Godhead, drunk with the Spirit. The conventional picture of Old Testament religion was that of a *break* with tradition, and little care was given to the continuity of beliefs within the history of the people of Israel.

The so-called Uppsala school, with its emphasis on oral tradition, forced a revision of the bookish method of composition that had been envisioned for the Old Testament.[11] Indeed there was now a tendency to over-emphasize oral transmission! But almost universally the role of oral tradition in the actual composition of a biblical book came to be recognized, and scholars began the study of *Traditionsgeschichte,* the "history of traditions,"—the formation and development of various corpora of traditions in Israel. This insight was applied to the Pentateuch on a large scale. The classical J,E,P, and D documents became traditions; they were not "written" in the eighth century B.C.—they were tending to assume their final form after a long history of transmission. This line of transmission provided the thread of historical continuity that scholars recognized; it explained how so much genuine historical coloring (e.g., in the patriarchal stories) could have

---

[11]Cf., e.g., E. Nielsen, *Oral Tradition* (Chicago, 1954).

been preserved in writings that were, after all, far removed in time from the events which they described. Thus the reality of a tradition, of a continuity of belief within the people of God, came to be admitted as never before, and the viewpoint was extended also to New Testament studies. Here the role of the Church in the composition of the New Testament was more clearly appreciated. On the basis of the scholarly studies of *Formgeschichte* (the study of literary types within the literature), there was even exaggeration; one spoke of the "creative" factor of the Church in the ongoing life of the traditions. But the undeniable gain is the fact that the concept of tradition has definitely entered into the scientific understanding of the life of Israel and the Church, and of the composition of the Bible.

We must recognize that the word "tradition" is often subject to ambiguity. It denotes sheerly oral tradition or also written tradition, both considered as a mode of transmission. Then it can also be applied to the things transmitted, the beliefs themselves. The very concept of tradition also goes beyond itself and points to a reality that transcends while it produces the word—the people of God itself, the society in which the tradition inheres.

From the point of view of ecumenism, the emphasis on tradition is a gain, provided that the biblical concept of tradition and the Catholic view of tradition as a classical "source of revelation" are not identified. Professor James Barr proclaimed this *caveat* at the 1964 Notre Dame University colloquium, and it is worth noting. The normative and methodological aspects of tradition in Catholic theology are absent from tradition in the biblical sense. The prophets, for example, freely develop and even transform the earlier data—as Ezechiel, who makes a travesty of the salvation history in his indictment of the nation's infidelity (cc. 16, 23), or Osee and Jeremiah, who cancel the Old Covenant. Similarly, the his-

101

torians, as the Deuteronomist (Jgs to Kgs) and the Chronicler (Ez-Neh, and 1-2 Par) transform in varying degrees the earlier material handed down. But the fact remains that tradition is a living reality within the People of God; there is no fixation on the mechanism of words. The contribution of this new insight, biblical tradition, to ecumenism lies in this: an appreciation of the community, and even of the *locus* of authority within the community of God's people.

The Catholic concept of tradition is undergoing serious revision which will have repercussions on theological methodology and the evaluation of tradition as a theological source. This problematic—the coinherence of Scripture and tradition —is pertinent, but cannot be discussed here.[12]

Has the traditional Protestant principle, *sola Scriptura,* yielded anything in the face of the new emphasis upon tradition? Several years ago Professor Floyd Filson expressed a logical conclusion of the Protestant principle: "Any Protestant who never tests or examines his own confession or that of his Church by the standard of Scripture, and who fails to keep clear what he believes and what his Church confesses is secondary to Scripture, is a Roman Catholic at heart. He is ascribing controlling authority to his Church and its tradition."[13] At the biblical session of the Protestant-Catholic symposium at Harvard University in March of 1963 this statement came up for discussion, and it was denied by some Protestant exegetes. One (Methodist) scholar admitted that he interpreted his Bible out of his Church's tradition; he was not, as he put it, a free-wheeling exegete. I think there is room for an extended explication of the Protestant hermeneutical principle of the Word (the Word *in* the communion

---

[12]See the discussion in G. Moran, *Scripture and Tradition* (New York, 1963).

[13]*Which Books Belong in the Bible* (Philadelphia, 1957), p. 164, as quoted in L. Alonso Schökel, *Understanding Biblical Research* (New York, 1963), p. 44.

of Saints?), and the future may reveal progress in this direction.[14]

Another area where scholars of varying persuasions have reached a measure of agreement is that of Old Testament cult. In the past exaggerations are to be found on both sides, dictated by the respective religious commitments. Apparently guided by a certain anti-sacramentalism, Protestants depreciated the cultic principle in Israel, despite the fact that it is securely embedded in Israelite law. And this prevented them from achieving a fuller appreciation of the Psalms (contrast H. Gunkel's "spiritual" evaluation of the Psalter with the liturgical stress of S. Mowinckel). On the whole, Catholics were more correct in upholding the cultic principle, even where this was dictated more by a favorable *Weltanschauung* than by an exegetical argument. Not many on either side were open to a totally frank evaluation of the judgment passed by the prophets on the temple sacrifices.

The words of the pre-exilic prophets (Am 5:21-27; Os 6:6; Mi 6:6-8; Is 1:11-17; Jer 6:20; 7:21-22) are clearly condemnatory of the sacrifices offered by Israel. Positively, other virtues are demanded: obedience, justice, etc. How is this tension to be resolved? Père de Vaux speaks of a "dialectical negation": not this, but that—in the sense of, not so much this, as that.[15] Already in the tradition of Samuel the principle was expressed: "obedience is better than sacrifice" (1 Sm 15:22). In other words, pure formalism is the object of condemnation; without an inner response, the liturgy will be in vain.

Nonetheless, it is not an exaggeration to say that the changed attitude to the liturgy in many Protestant circles is

---

[14]See the attention which R. McAfee Brown gives to tradition in the Protestant position, " 'Tradition' as a Problem for Protestants," *Union Seminary Quarterly Review* 16 (1960/61), pp. 197-221. See also G. Tavard, "The Holy Tradition," *Dialogue For Reunion,* ed. L. Swidler (New York, 1962), pp. 54-88.

[15]*Ancient Israel* (New York, 1961), pp. 454-456.

due to the advance in the correct understanding of the Old Testament polemics against sacrifice.

In recent times both Catholics and Protestants have rediscovered a branch of biblical studies where they find themselves in remarkable agreement: biblical theology. If we define this as the systematic organization in biblical categories of the biblical data concerning God and man, we remain on the level of historical description where agreement should be expected. As J. L. McKenzie has remarked, "Entire unanimity should be theoretically possible in exegesis itself; for the meaning of the Bible has been determined by its authors, not by its interpreters."[16] It is not surprising then, to find that the Old Testament theologies of W. Sichrodt, G. von Rad, E. Jacob, G. E. Wright and others are used extensively in Catholic circles. Significantly, the objections made to these interpretations derive not from differences in religious commitment, but from legitimate differences of opinion in the interpretation of biblical data. Thus, one may properly question if the concept of covenant is as central to Old Testament theology as Eichrodt makes it out to be, or if Wright's emphasis on the God who acts is not overdone. In these questions it is evidence and argument that decide the issue.

But when one leaves the area of straight historical description and analysis, there is less agreement. The question ceases to be what did it mean, and becomes, what *does* it mean.[17] The problem is then that of translating the biblical data into modern statement and categories, and the religious and philosophical stance of the person influences considerably his interpretation. At this point the historian of theology may rightly judge that the hermeneutical trends in the churches are going in directions opposed to each other. The most

---

16 Cf. the article cited in note 8, p. 199.

17This important distinction is drawn by K. Stendahl in "Biblical Theology," *The Interpreter's Dictionary of the Bible* (New York, 1962), I, pp. 413-432.

sophisticated and influential Protestant position is considerably influenced by German philosophy, in particular by Heidegger.[18] The Catholic position is also complex, due to the tension between Scripture and dogma which was indicated above. At times the Catholic exegesis which is offered for Catholic beliefs can only be described as pneumatic—that is, the exegesis offers little if any historical and rational support of the dogma in question. One is left simply with an insight of the Church into a given biblical passage (e.g., Genesis 3:15, or Luke 1:28, and Mariological doctrines). The eminent Dutch theologian, E. Schillebeeckx, O.P., practically admits this.[19] He describes Catholic dogma as a correct (but never exhaustive) hearing of some reality or word of revelation. The revelation is a constitutive part of the apostolic Church and it is continually being heard by the Church in its history. Hence the Bible has a double context: its historical, written context which is established by exegesis and biblical theology, and its contemporary context in a given period of the history of the Church, which is investigated by the dogmatic (or systematic) theologian. The later dogma is not found *as such* in the Bible. But since the Word of God in the Bible is to be *heard,* not only by Israel or the apostolic Church, but by all men, there are various levels of hearing. The biblical level is investigated by the exegete, and the historical level (in the life of the Church) is investigated by the dogmatic theologian, who listens to the Word and takes into account the hearing it has been given by the Church; then he attempts to formulate it with relevance for his time.

---

[18]See the summary article by R. E. Brown, S.S., "After Bultmann, What?—An Introduction to the Post-Bultmannians," *Catholic Biblical Quarterly* 26 (1964), pp. 1-30, and the essays edited by J. M. Robinson and J. B. Cobb, *The Later Heidegger and Theology* (New York, 1963).

[19]See his "Exegese, Dogmatik und Dogmenentwicklung," *Exegese und Dogmatik,* ed. H. Vorgrimler (Mainz, 1962), pp. 91-114, esp. pp. 96-101.

Some Catholic exegetes look to a theory of a "fuller sense"[20] of Scripture as an adequate explanation of how the Church "hears" the Word. On this view, the "pneumatic" exegesis is really the Church's insight into a biblical text whereby she finds a fuller meaning, which the text is seen to have in the light of later revelation. Enough has been said here to indicate that Catholic theological thought is still developing an understanding of its own methodology.

3. *The Biblical Movement and the Ecumenical Outlook Within the Church*

Of equal importance with the exegetical dialogue between Catholic and Protestant scholars is the effect of the biblical movement on ecumenism within the Church itself. The biblical renewal has been rightly considered a contribution to the ecumenical movement because anything that contributes to the renewal of the Church's life indirectly promotes ecumenism. Here we can point to certain areas where the new biblical orientation has already influenced the teaching of the Church and rendered it more intelligible and attractive to the modern man.

Genesis 1-3 can serve as an example for the new understanding which is enriching many levels of Catholic teaching. The most significant change is perhaps one of attitude. One no longer has recourse to these chapters as if they contained all the truth about creation—thus eliminating growth in the revelation of this truth throughout the biblical period—or as if they were a revealed description of the actual mode of creation. The discovery of the ancient creation myths of Mesopotamia was responsible for bringing this about, and for the resulting insight into the imaginative nature of the descriptions of Genesis. With this development went also a more

---

[20]Cf. R. E. Brown, S.S., "The *Sensus Plenior* in the Last Ten Years," *Catholic Biblical Quarterly* 25 (1963), pp. 262-285.

supple interpretation of individual verses; the formal, syllogistic approach to Genesis 2:7, which some theologians used
to polemicize against the theory of evolution, is no longer
operative. The anthropomorphic nature of the description of
the creation of man in 2:7 seems obvious now, and the recognition of this anthropomorphism has been extended also to
the creation of woman in 2:21. Here again, it is useless to
look for information concerning the manner of creation, as
though Eve were created materially from man's body; the
point of the narrative is that Eve is made of the same nature
as man.[21]

Heilsgeschichte, or salvation history, which seems to have
been used for the first time by a nineteenth-century Protestant
theologian, Johann C. K. Hofmann, has become a household
word in Catholic theology; it springs from preoccupation with
the biblical record. I understand by it the interpretation of
certain events in history as God's (saving) actions, and I
would point to the succinct presentations of salvation history
which are to be found in the liturgical formulas of Deuter-
onomy (e.g., 26:1-9) or of the Psalms (e.g., 135 [136]). In
a broad sense, of course, the entire Bible bears witness to the
unfolding of this history, which culminates in the redemptive
death, resurrection and ascension of Jesus. Subjectively, salvation history means the interpretation by faith, the response
of Israel and the Church to the intervention of God in man's
history. As a pedagogical approach, salvation history serves
as a unitive theme around which a study of the Bible can
revolve. Even more importantly, it provides a synthesis of
the Christian message which is concrete and living, as opposed
to a more rational, philosophical, and scholastic approach
which has characterized Catholic expositions heretofore. And
the more biblical the exposition, the more mutual will be the

---

[21]So the recent trend among dogmatic theologians, but T. J. Mother-
way, S.J., in *Chicago Studies* 1 (1960), pp. 115-132, voices the opposition of some theologians.

comprehension and understanding between the various Christian groups.

The importance of biblical terminology and of the biblical view of things has been high-lighted by Vatican Council II. The vote of the Fathers to consider the schema on the Blessed Virgin in the context of the Church is an example of a biblical approach which can expect a more sympathetic understanding from Protestants than might otherwise have been expected. Again, the emphasis on the Church as the "People of God" reflects the choice of a markedly biblical concept, within which the nature of the Church may be fruitfully analysed. In the Old Testament the concept of the People (*ᶜam* = LXX, *laos*) has a remarkable development. It points in the first instance to the bond that united Israel as the covenanted and elected of Yahweh (Ex 19:4-7; Dt 4 & 7; 32:8ff.). But it carries with it a note of tension, which is supplied by the prophets (Os 1:9): judgment, under the demands of God—and also glorification, under the promise of God (Zach 2:14-16). It becomes a favorite phrase of the early Church (especially in Saint Paul), to express its consciousness of itself as the fulfillment of the Old Testament promises, the true Israel, which paradoxically has been formed by the inclusion of the "nations" who had not been God's People. This designation, therefore, has rich biblical associations that belong to all who share in the biblical traditions, and it forms a common ground to enter into dialogue.

Much more might be said, particularly with reference to New Testament studies, about the biblical rapprochement between Catholics and non-Catholics. This may suffice as an index to the progress made among Old Testament scholars. In conclusion, two things need to be kept in mind. Catholic-Protestant dialogue on a theological level has hardly scratched the surface in this country. We are far behind our German brethren; German theologians have been meeting ever since 1946 and discussing their theological differences. This does not mean that union can be achieved by theologians, but it will not be achieved without theological discussion. Secondly, there remains a great deal of theological homework for Catholic scholars to perform. In particular, the relation of Scripture to tradition, Bible to Dogma, has to be worked out, not merely theoretically, but on the practical level of critical methodology.

JUDAISM, SCRIPTURES, AND ECUMENISM[1]

by

Steven S. Schwarzschild

The Specifically Christian Character of Ecumenism

For the Jew the denotations of the terms "Scriptures" and "ecumenism" require explicit clarification.

"Ecumenism" designates that movement in Christendom, launched by Protestants in the World Council of Churches, for example, and currently high on the agenda of the Roman-Catholic Vatican Council, which seeks to lend unity to all those who, though separated in various ecclesiastical institutions and by divergent theological beliefs, share a common faith in Jesus as savior and in the New Testament as holy scriptures. The specifically Christian nature of ecumenism makes it, then, self-evident that Judaism and the people of Israel have no place in this movement. And in fact the names of all ecumenical bodies, conferences, and publications express abundantly and correctly that ecumenism is a concern of Christians, and only of Christians,—of Protestants, Roman-Catholics, Eastern Orthodoxy, and other Christian communicants. As Jews we are, ought to be, and always will be outsiders to these endeavors, for we adhere to not one of ecumenism's indispensable premises. We cannot and will not endorse any of its aims for ourselves,—other than, of course, to pray that the search for divine truth and human concord as it is pursued by any and all of our fellow-men may be crowned with blessing and success.

These facts directly lead to some neglected conclusions with respect to the chapter on the proper attitude of Roman-Catholics to the Jews that has been proposed at the Vatican

---

[1]This paper has also been published in *Judaism,* Summer 1964.

111

Council.[2] We are reliably informed that the so-called liberal elements at the Council favored, while the more conservative elements in and outside of the Roman Curia opposed, the passage of the chapter on the Jews altogether, or at least fought its inclusion in the schema on ecumenism. It has now been officially announced that it will be considered as a completely discrete statement.[3] Roman-Catholic "liberals" evi-

---

[2]Its original text and English translations have by now appeared in various places. It is noteworthy that its chief New Testament proof-text is Eph. 2:14-17, the same text used by Markus Barth in his (Protestant) discussion of this subject (*cf.* footnote 11). Everything said about the implications of this viewpoint in discussing Barth thus also applies to the Vatican Council document: the unification of mankind "in Christ" and by "breaking down the wall of the law and commandments" is, of course, basic to the Christian faith but entirely incomprehensible and unacceptable to the Jewish; and the "evangelistic" overtones of such a phrase as "Although a large part of the chosen people remains separated from Christ . . ." are both unmistakable as well as, from the Jewish point of view, to be in every way declined.—I must, at this point, put it on the record that in all of the following I speak only for myself, and for no other person and no Jewish institution. I have, naturally, discussed the questions with which I deal with a number of authoritative Jewish religious and organizational leaders, however. And I also must add the *caveat* that nothing that I say is intended to criticize the views or actions of Christians as such; they obviously have the right and even the duty to formulate their wishes and hopes in conformity with their own beliefs, not in accordance with mine; I desire merely to formulate my Jewish thinking, both as a reaction to Christian predilections and as indigenously Jewish, and to submit it for whatever attention it may evoke.

[3]Cf. New York *Times,* May 18, 1964, pp. 1f. This paper was written and read long before the Vatican announcement of the establishment of a new Secretariat for non-Christians and of the separation of the chapter on the Jews from its original ecumenical context. The new developments are, from the Jewish point of view, highly to be welcomed. In some significant respects they put into reality what was asked for in this study. But in the most fundamental respects the situation remains, and is bound to remain, unaltered. Even the new office and statement will, of course, retain an underlying proselytizing goal: the Roman-Catholic faith wishes to be regarded as the *patria communis*—"without renouncing the church's traditional desire to take in ever larger segments of mankind," though "evangelical intent will not be overt." (As *Commonweal* put it in an editorial of May 29, 1964: "How can the pilgrim help but feel himself a stranger if he is told that Rome, rather than his own spiritual homeland, is his real country? And is he likely, in the first place, to think of himself as a 'pilgrim'?") indeed, the newly independent statement on the Jews is still to "be shepherded through the Council by the Secretariat for Christian

dently regretted this development, and numerous "official" Jewish voices expressed their ardent hope that the statement, in some form, would be passed at the next session of the Council. From our delineation of the inappositeness of ecumenism correctly understood on the one hand and Judaism on the other, it follows that the "conservatives" were, in fact, quite right: certainly from the Jewish point of view, and presumably also from the Christian, Israel and Judaism as such have no place in a schema on Christian ecumenism.

At least three other considerations buttress this conclusion. A Protestant observer at the Vatican Council, Kyle Haselden, has made the equivalent judgment even with respect to what was originally the fifth chapter in the schema on ecumenism which deals with religious liberty[4]:

> Through several bishops the Secretariat for Promoting Christian Unity strongly championed the inclusion of religious liberty in the ecumenism schema. But to this reporter it appears that the stronger the argument for embracing religious liberty by the schema on ecumenism

Unity." (No doubt, this is merely a bureaucratic left-over.)—And the unintelligent and undignified reaction of "official" Jewish, civic voices —about which we will speak later—is also unaffected. The original report in the *Times* included this astounding paragraph: "Some doubts were expressed in informed circles as to whether World Judaism [what is that?] would welcome a change that seemed to minimize the Judeo-Christian connection through the Old Testament and place Judaism on a par with all other world religions in Catholic eyes." Sure enough, the *National Jewish Post and Opinion* (March 22, 1964) features a report above its masthead which begins with the words: "The Vatican has taken two steps which would appear to adversely affect its relations with world Jewry." These Jewish politicians' objections are, of course, completely invalid: Islam, for one, is as much bound to the Bible as is Christianity and is doctrinally and culturally considerably closer to Judaism than is Christianity. And why, by heaven, should Jews want to be singularly identified with Western Christian culture in the apocalyptic age of the Occident, of Auschwitz and Hiroshima, and in the age in which Africans, Asians, "Black Muslims" and Californian Zen Buddhists make rigorous efforts to dissociate themselves from and actively rebel against White civilization?

[4]*The Christian Century*, Dec. 18, 1963. This, too, has been carried out meanwhile. (*Cf.* footnote 3.)

became, the greater appeared the reasons for dealing with religious liberty independently. Certainly, as Cardinal Ritter said, religious liberty is "a basic and pre-requisite for ecumenical contacts with other Christian bodies. . . . Without such a declaration, mutual confidence will be impossible and serious dialogue will be precluded." But religious liberty is not merely a means to unity; it is valid in itself as a means of faith. Religious liberty not only preconditions men to unity; it also enables man to be man. The subject belongs, then, not in the schema on ecumenism nor, as proposed by some, in the catch-all Schema Seventeen on the presence of the church in the world but, theologically at least, it belongs in a schema or chapter on the nature of man.

What Haselden wrote about the chapter on religious liberty applies to the section on the relations with the Jews. Indeed, it applies with even greater force, for to Christians ecumenism, as correctly defined, is a matter not of proselytism but of unification, and, therefore, though perhaps not the best at least a valid reason for religious liberty; when, on the other hand, ecumenism is referred to Jews, it inevitably has proselytizing implications,—and any Christian attitude toward Jews that is part of an ecumenical context, however moral otherwise, must, therefore, be suspect. Fortunately, an increasing number of religiously responsible Jewish spokesmen have drawn attention to these considerations in recent months —foremost among them Rabbi Joseph B. Soloveitchik, surely one of the most influential Jewish guides of our time.[5]

That Jews should be concerned with proselytizing implications and overtones in Christian "ecumenical" approaches to them can hardly be surprising in view of two-thousand years of Christian endeavors in "the mission to the Jews"—by spiritual exertion, by stealth and by bloody force—, in view of the agony of the body of the Jewish people in our own time

---

[5] *Cf. Day-Morning Journal* (Yiddish), Feb. 5, 1964.

at the hands of nations which were at least nominally Christian, and in view of actual explicit statements such as those of Msgr. John Oesterreicher, the head of the Institute of Judaeo-Christian Studies. The latter is centrally involved in the current Vatican Council deliberations regarding the Jewish people. He is also a Jewish apostate and, therefore, doubly a person of spiritual concern to Jews. He has said that "whether we will or no, we are missioners at all times. . . . We will win [the Jews] if we move on the height to which we are called. . . ."[6]

Fr. Gregory Baum (another Jewish apostate turned Roman-Catholic ecumenist) has given his reasons for wishing the chapter on the Jews included in the schema on ecumenism[7]: first because Christians are spiritually related to the "old Israel"; second, the division between baptized Jews and unbaptized Jews is symbolic of all other schisms in the church; and third, because of the Christian eschatological hope of the conversion of the Jews. Clearly, Fr. Baum's reasons are explicitly or implicitly missionary—or else they are somewhat flimsy homilies.

It is inevitable and, from their point of view, perfectly legitimate and even spiritually necessary that the Roman-Catholic approach to the Jews should be essentially missionary in character. And this is characteristic not only of Roman-Catholics but of Protestants as well. Among the latter this is best discerned not among those who are actively engaged in "the mission to the Jews" but precisely among the few who have of late strongly opposed this ancient Christian enterprise. Even more than the famous statement of Reinhold

---

[6]*The Apostolate to the Jews,* vol. 6, no. 4, pp. 82f.

[7]Quoted by Rabbi Arthur Gilbert of the National Conference of Christians and Jews in "The Council and the Jews," *The Reconstructionist,* Jan. 10, 1964, p. 9.—This is a rather typical combination: the "Roman-Catholic" involved is a Jewish apostate, and the Jew is a functionary of one of the "civic organizations" about which we will still have to say a word or two.

Niebuhr,[8] Markus Barth is a good case in point. His argument runs something like this[9] : the so-called "mission to the Jews" must be abandoned. What Christian could arrogate to himself the right condescendingly to approach the Jews who, by God's election, wittingly or unwittingly, gladly or rebelliously, are themselves the divine missionaries? The Christian owes the Jew nought but "testimony" through his humility, through his prayer for forgiveness, and through full understanding of the Jew's right, work, and even his rebellion. Instead of "the mission to the Jews," he should speak of "the indebtedness to the Jews" (*Schuld an die Juden*), which includes the guilt toward them. Barth praises the new church order of the Nederlandsche Hervormde Kerk (Dutch Reformed Church) which calls for the "conversation [or dialogue] with Israel," and he regrets that the 1954 World Council of Churches in Evanston in effect rejected this view of the matter.

But we must clearly understand that Barth does not really abandon the Christian desire to bring Israel to Jesus—no believing Christian could; he merely suggests a new and perhaps better way of achieving the same end: ". . . only after the Jews have found reason to ask about the unexpected friendliness toward them will come the time and the opportunity to speak to them of 'Jesus of Nazareth, the king of the Jews.' . . . Conversion of the Jews to Christianity? Under no circumstances—after all the falsehood and evil that have been inflicted on the Jews in the name of Christianity. But conversion to Christ, to the Father, to the Holy Ghost."[10]

---

[8]"The Relations of Christians and Jews in Western Civilization," *Central Conference of American Rabbis Journal*, April, 1958, pp. 18-32.

[9]*The Broken Wall—A Study of the Epistle to the Ephesians*, Chicago, 1959, esp. pp. 123-136, and *Israel und die Kirche im Briefe des Paulus an die Epheser, Theologische Existenz Heute*, no. 75, Munich, 1959.

[10] This is much more a Barthian rejection of the "ism" of "Christianity" in favor of the reality of "Christ" than it is a rejection of "the mission to the Jews."

The same fundamental goal is implied in the crucial text from Ephesians (2:14f.) from which Barth takes the title of his book: all mankind, white and black, Jew and gentile, is to be united under the aegis of Jesus; and, note well, the wall which must be broken so that this end can be attained is primarily the very Law of God to which the Jew is eternally and sacredly covenanted: "For he is our peace, who has made us both one, and *has broken down the dividing wall* of hostility *by abolishing* in his flesh *the law of commandments and ordinances. . . .*"[11]

One must not take exception to the Christian desire to convert Israel. This is perfectly understandable to us for several reasons: our understanding of and respect for the sincerity of Christianity; our belief in "the free market-place of ideas"; the consideration that every monotheistic and, therefore, monistic truth must seek to persuade all men of its veracity and goodness; and the analogy which we draw with Judaism, which itself looks forward to the messianic day when all the nations will "go up from year to year to worship the King, the Lord of hosts," and when "the Lord shall be king over all the earth; in that day shall the Lord be one and His name one" (Zech. 14:9, 16). On the other hand, Jews can surely not be expected to welcome or endorse their own proselytization. That some Roman-Catholics might, therefore, want the chapter on the Jews included in the schema on ecumenism is one thing; that some Jews and liberals pressed for it can, from the Jewish point of view, be regarded at best as incomprehension and at worst as folly.

The same tenor—which Rabbi Soloveitchik has called "evangelistic"—is unmistakable in the published draft-text of the originally proposed Vatican Council statement about the Jews. A due respect for Christian theology requires that we be quite outspoken about it. What the statement says about

---

[11]Again, notice the coincidence of Barth's reasoning with that of the proposed Vatican Council chapter; *cf.* footnote 2.

the relationship between Christianity and the people of Israel and about the sinfulness of antisemitism is in no wise new; it merely restates what has long been the more enlightened Christian view and reiterates that the Hebrew Bible and its believers are no more though also no less than the lower stratum of divine truth on which the higher level of the New Testament and its chief figure rise. The text does not absolve the Jews of the crime of "deicide." It rather spreads the guilt to *all* sinners. The very term "deicide" and the proposition that the crucifixion is enacted whenever a sin is committed imply a doctrine that is fundamental to the Christian faith but which is, of course, totally unacceptable to the Jewish community, namely that Jesus is God. Publicity has highlighted the proposed comparative exculpation of the Jewish people of one single execution. At a time when the question of the moral involvement of Christendom in the slaughter of six-million Jews and unnumbered earlier martyrs has again become an issue of world-wide soul-searching, Jews should surely be careful to weigh the implications of Christian "absolution" of one death. Indeed, the question of the crucifixion has to be pushed one theological step further: Christian and Jewish theologies are not primarily interested in a mere incident in ancient penology; what is at stake is truly central: the acceptance or rejection of one who claims messiahship, divinity, and the power of salvation. From both vantage-points, the answer to the real question at hand may, then, have to turn out quite differently from what people of good will usually tend to think.[12] Jews cannot buy the safety of their bodies at the price of their souls' deepest truth.

---

[12]*Cf.* my paper "Rosenzweig on Judaism and Christianity," *Conservative Judaism*, Winter, 1956, pp. 41-48.—The argument of Dr. James Daane in "The Anatomy of Antisemitism" in *Christianity Today* which aroused so much "official" Jewish resentment is, after all, far from completely invalid: the Jews are condemned, in the Christian view, not because of their role in the crucifixion but because they reject the gospel message; and, in the second place, the fate of the central figure in the New Testament is to the Christian the fate of God incarnate, while to the Jew it is the fate of a man.

The allusion to the theme and problem of "The Deputy" requires something else to be said at this point. In a way this is the worst of all possible times to raise the question of Jewish-Christian relations. It is no coincidence that the two questions, the crucifixion and the European-Jewish holocaust, have come to the fore at the same time. They are historically and psychologically connected: the pope who now presides over the Vatican Council was Cardinal Secretary of State under Pope Pius XII and is mentioned, though only in passing, in the play's documentary appendix. He has felt impelled to exonerate his predecessor-once-removed on several occasions, once as he was about to leave what he did not explicitly acknowledge to be Israeli soil. That the second session of the Vatican Council ended in an unproductive draw was admitted in so popular and respectful a medium as *Time* magazine. The suspicion that Paul VI's trip to the Holy Land was a diversion from this fact lies near at hand. And that the ambiguous "openings" to the Jewish people are an attempt to cover up the deep-seated moral and historical resentments between Jews and Roman-Catholics can hardly be gainsaid: at the present time, whenever a harsh word is about to be said about Jewish-Christian relations, the publicity-conscious spokesmen of both sides immediately warn that it may have injurious effects on the burgeoning new friendship.

The situation is really rather hopeless at this historical juncture. With the exception of the diminutively few active anti-Nazi fighters, the European gentile-Christian is in an inextricable moral fix. If he does not confess his guilt and repent, he is either unregenerate, or in effect perpetuating the crime of silence, or else even today spiritually straddling the fence; if, on the other hand, he does confess his guilt, the sensitive Jew wonders a) whether the unimaginable crime can really be retroactively mitigated so easily; b) whether the contrition is genuine; and c) whether demonstrative, visible shame is not bound to be a mixture of "grandstanding" and sentimentality. (Whenever a German I meet does not speak about the one great outstanding issue between us, I inwardly seethe about his callousness; but if he does, I wince resentfully under his attempt to talk, whether honestly or disingenuously, about something that cannot really be the object of mere words.)

Between Jews and Christians this is perhaps the time for silence, as it was the time to speak up twenty-five years ago. After the storm is over—if it is over—, nature, like the spirit, needs a long moment to catch its breath, to put things into proper perspective, to gather its wits, to contemplate the reality of the situation, to assess the damage that was done, to consider the individual's position in the new scheme of things. A generation from now the pieces may fall into place, and our view of them may have cleared. Right now, our Egypt is barely behind us, and the Promised Land is still far away. We are the generation of the desert, no longer willing to live under the slave-master, not yet ready for freedom, certainly incapable of easy fraternization between master and liberated slave. The biblical generation of the desert, including its greatest leaders, had to die before the next stage of history could begin. As for Egypt, to be sure, "it will swear unto the Lord of hosts . . . there will be an altar unto the Lord in the midst of the land of Egypt and a memorial unto the Lord by its border. It shall be a sign and a witness unto the Lord of hosts in the land of Egypt, for they will cry unto the Lord because of oppressors, and He will send them a savior, and a defender, who will rescue them. The Lord will be known to Egypt, and Egypt will know the Lord. . . . They will serve with sacrifice and offering, and they will vow a vow unto the Lord and fulfill it. The Lord will smite Egypt, smite and heal, and they will return unto the Lord, and He will be entreated and heal them. . . . Israel will be third with Egypt and Assyria, a blessing in the midst of the land. For the Lord of hosts will bless him saying: 'Blessed be My people Egypt, and the work of My hands Assyria, and My inheritance Israel'" (Is. 19:18-25). But this biblical promise is interlaced no less than six times with the qualifying phrase: "On that day." Let it be the messianic day; let it be tomorrow; it is not and cannot be today.

A negative evaluation of the proposed Vatican statement is bound to shock many well-meaning people. It must come as a surprise to them after all the laudatory and grateful Jewish reactions and, indeed, after the strenuous Jewish organizational efforts to have it drafted and adopted. What has to be understood is that a considerable number of Jews—including rabbis and scholars—continue to suffer from the age-old memories of Jewish persecutions caused by the accusation of deicide; any promise to cancel or to weaken this accusation offers them wondrous relief. They are not very much concerned with whether this chapter, which they mistakenly welcome, is passed in one context or another. All they desire is its surest and earliest passage. By and large, however, it has not been rabbis or scholars but civic organizations and individuals that have been actively concerned with this entire matter—*i.e.,* not those primarily concerned with the truths and laws of Judaism but those who think in terms of the social, political, and physical welfare of Jewry, who are concerned with the sociological rather than the theological aspirations of Jews. They are often uninformed and even unconcerned with the faith of Israel, and to them the relationship between Jews and Christians as religious people is of the same order of significance as the anti-Jewish discrimination practiced by a golf-club or a "gentlemen's agreement" in a wealthy Detroit suburb. These Jewish "Madison Avenue" agencies are well financed, operate smoothly in the public arena and in smoke-filled conference-rooms, and in effect determine much of the "line" that sets the tone of what constitutes Jewish public opinion. Men like Rabbi Soloveitchik and Israeli chief-rabbi Nissim, on the other hand, have been

121

careful to give the Vatican Council plans no support. To assume that the resultant public image is a correct representation of the religious Jewish attitude is a miscalculation comparable, perhaps, to learning Roman-Catholic dogma from a poll of the local Knights of Columbus on a Saturday night or to deducing Protestant theology from invocations delivered at political rallies.

The Stumbling Block of Scriptures

We turn to "Scriptures," the second term in the title. Scriptures obviously hold a central place in the total ecumenical movement, because about them revolves the entirety of the Christian faith and, therefore, of Christian unity. It is widely believed that clearing up difficulties and divergencies in the derivation of doctrine and authority from Scriptures will eventually resolve the disagreements among Christians. Whether or not this assumption is correct, it is by no means easy to determine exactly what the term "Scriptures" means even for Christians. The internal Christian discussions about the possibility of producing a Bible-translation acceptable to both Protestants and Catholics are only one indication of this lack of accord.[13] There are controversies about the apocryphal books. There are different numberings of commandments and Psalms. There is canon 1391 requiring all Roman-Catholic Bibles to be printed with footnotes (the

---

[13]The most extraordinary aspect of this search for a common translation is the wide-spread assumption, even among otherwise sophisticated theologians, that "scientific" Bible-study lifts us to an "objective" level beyond philosophical or denominational pre-conceptions. (*Cf.* Thomas Corbishley, S.J., Fr. Eugene H. Maly, Cardinal Cushing in "The Common Bible," *The Dialogue,* Bulletin no. 26, Oct., 1963, National Conference of Christians and Jews, Fr. Walter M. Abbott, pp. 3f., 8.) Of course, positivistic, scientist premises themselves constitute an antecedent and determinative frame of reference, and one that is the more dangerous for being often unadmitted or unconscious. This is also true of the new Jewish Publications Society of America Bible translation.

counterpart to the Jewish doctrine that the Oral Torah is of one piece with the Written, which is to say that authoritative commentary, or Tradition, is an integral part of Revelation). And there are many other divergencies. Bernard Cardinal Alfrink of Utrecht therefore concluded: "I find here no solution except that one group should sacrifice its own idiom and make use of the other's idiom. A compromise is not possible."[14] And yet there is, of course, some basic agreement among Christians as to what constitutes Scriptures. Otherwise, neither the hopeful discussions about a common translation nor even the faintest expectation of ecumenical success would be conceivable. For all Christians, "Old Testament" and New Testament constitute the substance of divine Revelation.

If, then, the term "Scriptures" is by no means free of ambiguities and difficulties even for Christians, this is true *a fortiori* as between Jews and Christians. There are details, such as the order of books, the numberings of chapters and verses, correct translations and interpretations, *et al.,* even of the so-called "Old Testament" which we are supposed to share —and in some measure, of course, do share. The one great and insuperable partion between Jews and Christians is what happens after the Hebrew Bible. On that decisive question turns literally everything else. For Jews, "Scripture" is Torah, and Torah comprises not only the twenty-four books of the Hebrew canon but also the *torah shebe'al peh,* the Oral Torah, the Talmud and all its vast ramifications. The Written and the Oral Torah are, as we have said, of one piece in Jewish teaching; they were both revealed together at Mount Sinai; they are of equal divine dignity; and Tradition—a synonym in Judaism for Talmudic teaching—if anything surpasses in authority the Bible itself. After all, it is Tradition (in Christianity incidentally as much as in Judaism) which

---

[14]*Twelve Council Fathers,* Fr. Walter M. Abbott, S.J., New York, 1963.

determines what constitutes the canonical as over against the uncanonical books of Scriptures.[15] It is hardly necessary to describe the immense doctrinal, legal, spiritual and ethical differences which result from these respective Jewish and Christian definitions of what the term "Scriptures" means.

Positive "Ecumenical" Possibilities

Neither ecumenism, which is an exclusively Christian endeavor, nor Scriptures, about the nature of which we substantially disagree, can bind together Christian and Jew. This is the nadir of our consideration of Christian-Jewish relations. From here, the path can be only upward. And it would be impious, uncharitable, willfully obstructionist, and simply unrealistic to close our eyes to the fact that, for all the differences that inevitably separate us, we do, after all, possess common ground in the Bible. This common ground is of supreme importance to us both. Its extent is this: Everything that Jews regard as divine written Revelation (disregarding some relatively minor matters) is also held sacred by Christians, though not everything that Christians regard as divine Revelation is accepted by Jews. It would obviously be a disservice to the cause of Christian ecumenism to have the internal Christian dialogue concentrate on the apocryphal books which are in dispute between Roman-Catholics and Protestants; it is the common Christian biblical patrimony that must serve as the basis for rapprochement. Just so, the facts of the case would suggest that the efforts toward growing understanding between Christians and Jews and in the common search for truth should begin by leaving aside, at least for the moment, those portions of our respective *sancta* about which we disagree and concentrating on those which we share. In

---

[15]Cf. *Judaism Eternal—Selected Essays from the Writings of Rabbi Samson Raphael Hirsch,* ed. Dayan I. Gruenfeld, London, 1956, vol. 1, p. 102.

plain English, this means that Scriptures can serve as the platform of Jewish-Christian dialogue only if and when Christians are prepared to direct their hearts and minds to the exclusive canon of the Hebrew Bible—and Jews can only pray that this invitation will not appear to be a demand for an *a priori* theological self-immolation on the part of Christians. It would not be as self-abnegating a course of action as might at first appear. In the first place, it is nought but a methodological device applied to the Jewish-Christian dialogue, not a doctrinal commitment; besides, is it not part of Christian doctrine that the New Testament grows out of and fulfills the "Old"? One might thus say that, in following this procedure, the Christian would merely be retracing, as it were, the course of what he believes to be the inherent dialectic of the self-revelation of God.

To be sure, this sounds easier than it is. It is true that no one who believes in the Bible can very well refuse to heed any part of what he grants to be Scriptures. But the Scriptures to whose study the Jew can issue an invitation are not merely the literal and mechanical texts of certain commonly accepted books of the Hebrew Bible. Jewish Scriptures also include Tradition, or, again in plain English: Talmud—which, for the non-Jew, would at least have to be hypothetically relevant. (Reuchlin and other Reformers studied even Kabbalah.) Several reasons make such a view of the matter both necessary and possible.

Even if we pass over the conclusive evidence for the mutual interdependence and inter-wovenness of Bible and Talmud, it must be recognized that if "Scriptures" is limited to the twenty-four books of the *Tanach*, we will fall prey to a mechanical and fundamentalist Karaism that makes of the Bible not the vital, continuously inspired and inspiring Word of God that it is but a magical grab-bag of arbitrary human self-assertion. Instead of being guided by the Holy Spirit to the meaning, intention, and application of the Bible, we would be setting up our own criteria for selecting which section of the Bible is to become operative in our lives at any given moment and for how this section is to be interpreted. In short, Biblicism is actually (and contrary to its self-description) a form of humanism. *Sola Scriptura* has always led to a new and willful legalism of its own, whether with the Saducees, the Karaites, with Christians in general or Protestants in particular. The history of Roman-Catholic canon law and the development of Protestant legalism—in Calvinist Switzerland, Puritan New England, or in the German Lutheran synods—are telling evidence. Jewish doctrine, on the other hand, discerns the seeds of post-biblical law in the Bible itself, and it considers the hermeneutic methods as well as their results enshrined in the original act of Revelation.

This circumstance makes "ecumenical" dialogue between Jews and Christians both easier and more difficult. It is easier in that, from the Jewish point of view, the Christian is asked no more than to return to his own sources, to the Bible and to nothing else—but, be it well understood, Bible in the sense of *Torah*, that is : the Bible with all its infinite ramifications, written as well as oral. It is more difficult in that the entire Tradition of Judaism is ultimately submitted to the non-Jew as part and parcel of the source of faith and truth. Even as Christians invite one another to submit to the discipline of Scriptures in their search for unity, so the Jew must ask the Christian to spend the rest of his life in the study of rabbinic Judaism, the Judaism of the Pharisees rather than of anyone else as the legitimate interpreters and executors of the Word of God.

Admittedly, this is a truly utopian program. If Jewish-Christian understanding and mutual respect, and if the salvation of non-Jews, were to depend on the immediate realization of this hope, we should obviously have to await eschatological fulfillment before events on this order could be expected. Let it be clear that, eschatologically, this is indeed the faith of Israel: that "in the end of days the mountain of the Lord's house will be established as the top of the mountains and elevated above the hills, and all the nations will flow toward it. Many nations will say: 'Come, let us ascend to the mountain of the Lord, to the house of the God of Jacob, so that He may teach us of His ways, and we will walk in His paths, for from Zion goes forth Torah and the word of the Lord from Jerusalem . . .'" (Is. 2:2f.). Judaism emphatically believes the divine promise that in the messianic fulfillment all the nations of the world will be joined and will become naturalized ("supernaturalized") in the people of Israel and its true service of God. "Though His goodness and mercy and loving kindness are with Israel, His right hand is always stretched out to receive all those who come into the world . . . , as it is said: 'Unto Me every knee shall bend, every tongue shall swear' (Is. 45:23). For this confession from the gentiles the Holy One is waiting."[16] The classic Jewish confession of faith, Deut. 6:4, is interpreted as follows: "He is our God by making His name particularly attached to us; but He is also the one God of all mankind. He is our God in this world; He will be the only God in the world-to-come, as it is said: 'And the Lord shall be King over all the earth. In that day there shall be one God, and His name shall be one'" (Zech. 14:9).[17] This Zechariah quotation and Zeph. 3:9 are the Jewish *loci classici* of the doctrine of the universal acceptance of the law of the Torah.[18] These words of Zechariah bring to a climax the great messianic prayer with which every Jewish worship service ends.[19]

---

[16]*Mechilta,* 38b; *Midrash Tehillim,* 100, 1.

[17]*Mechilta,* 102a; *Sifre,* 73a.

[18]*Cf.* my "The Messianic Doctrine in Contemporary Jewish Thought," in *Great Jewish Ideas, B'nai B'rith Great Books Series,* vol. V, ed. A. E. Millgram, 1964, pp. 237-259.

[19]*Cf.* the moving description of the linkage between Jewish "particularism" and "universalism" in J. D. H. Soloveitchik, "What is My Beloved More than Any Other," (Hebrew) *Hadoar,* 9 Tishri 5724 (1963), p. 752.

The legitimacy of Christian proselytism with respect to the Jews has already been alluded to. We appreciate the good intentions of contemporary Christian theologians such as Reinhold Niebuhr and Markus Barth who have advocated the abandonment of such efforts.[20] But it is difficult to understand how anyone committed to a monotheistic—and monistic —truth can entertain the notion that two at least somewhat different truths can have ultimate status for mankind. If the Christian were to abandon the hope of converting the Jew and the Jew were to do the same with respect to the Christian, the almost inevitable conclusion would have to be that neither has full faith in his own religious commitment or that he does not value his fellow-man as equally entitled and obligated to truth and righteousness. The ultimate definition of ecumenism is, surely, the expectation of embracing all the children of men in the one single divine truth.[21]

The question is not the legitimacy of proselytism as such but its methods and the status of the unconverted prior to his eventual conversion. The Jew has millennial experience in the Christian and Moslem worlds with proselytism by stealth, by seduction, pressure, torture, and murder, as well as by persuasion and example. It is to these means of proselytism that he objects as morally and religiously illegitimate, not to proselytism itself. On the other hand, he also reserves for himself the right to engage in proselytism in turn.

Jewish proselytism is nothing new. Christians should be aware of it, if from nowhere else, from Matthew 23:15 which

---

[20]Franz Rosenzweig is generally held to have taught a Jewish doctrine of "the two covenants," but in my essay on Rosenzweig (*loc. cit.*) I have tried to show the invalidity of this belief.

[21]A Christian theologian suggests that this exclusive dichotomy is not necessary. With touching sincerity he says that we can leave the judgment of our respective truths to the ultimate verdict of God, and abstain, meanwhile, from infringing on another man's spiritual integrity. This may be true, and it is certainly an admirably restrained attitude. But we cannot hide the fact that, underlying such a view, must still be the hope and confidence that God's judgment will prove to justify our truth, not someone else's.

gives clear, albeit indirect, evidence of it.[22] Indeed, the relative abatement of Jewish missionary efforts in the last millennium-and-a-half is largely the effect of ancient and mediaeval antisemitic legislation in the Christian and Moslem worlds. At the present time there is renewed interest in missionary activities in certain Jewish circles in Israel and in this country. What Jewish law does insist on most emphatically is that converts to Judaism must be received only on the strength of their own convictions and commitment, that they must be attracted by Jewish example and general teaching, never by pressure of any kind, that they must be initially discouraged rather than urged on, and that conversion must be made altogether difficult so as to insure a completely voluntary and authentic act.

We come here to the ultimate ecumenical strategy of Judaism. Judaism proclaims a fundamental theological monism. But at the same time, the ecumenism of Jewish universalism is obviously an essentially eschatological expectation and largely inoperative in the interim. It might, therefore, seem as though non-Jews would remain in a state of perdition until the messianic unification of mankind under the banner of the Torah has been achieved. This would be tantamount to a doctrine of *extra synagogam nullum salus est.* But that is decidedly not the case. It is established and authoritative Jewish doctrine that "the righteous of all the nations of the world have their share in the world-to-come."[23] Jewish law defines in some detail who these "righteous of the nations of the world" are that can attain to salvation without holding the faith or practicing the law of Judaism. They are those non-Jews (*i.e.,* people who are neither born of a Jewish mother nor at any time converted to Judaism) who obey the so-called "seven commandments of the sons of

---

[22]*Cf.* in general, B. J. Bamberger, *Proselytism in the Talmudic Period,* Cincinnati, 1939; W. G. Braude, *Jewish Proselyting in the First Centuries of the Common Era* . . . , Providence, 1940.

[23]*B. Sanhedrin* 105a; *Tosefta Sanh.,* ch. 13:2; etc.

Noah," or the "Noachite commandments," which prohibit idolatry, the improper use of the name of God, murder, sexual immorality, and theft, and add the injunction to establish law and courts, and the prohibition against eating meat from a living animal.[24] These commandments are called "Noachite" because they are rabbinically deduced from Scriptures themselves, although there is some disagreement as to how many were originally issued to Adam and to Noah respectively. Yet, since both Adam and Noah are each the father of all mankind, from each of whom all the nations and all the races are descended, a covenant made with the family of each and either is binding on the entire human race. The Sinaitic covenant was between God and Israel alone, but the Noachitic covenant applies to all men. It comprises only what might be called the basic moral code for all human beings. Any non-Jew who abides by this law fully obeys the commandments addressed to him and shares with the Jew the promise of God's eternal salvation.

In the technical, canon-legal Jewish literature about this problem, one of the major points of discussion is that Maimonides, in his authoritative code, adds a requirement that only such Noachites fall heir to "their share in the world-to-come" as accept and obey the seven Noachite laws on the theological ground that they were revealed to Moses on Sinai.[25] Maimonides is in effect arguing that, apart from other points, the Noachitic covenant is not identical with any so-called "natural law."[26] He is also laying it down that

---

[24]*Cf.* Maimonides' *Mishneh Torah,* "Laws of the Kings," ch. 9:1.
[25]*Ibid.,* ch. 8:10f. *Cf.* my study "Do Noachites Have to Believe in Revelation? (A Passage in Dispute between Maimonides, Spinoza, Mendelssohn, and H. Cohen) A Contribution to a Jewish View of Natural Law," *Jewish Quarterly Review,* LII, no. 4, and LIII, no. 1.
[26]The New Testament also knows something of the Noachite covenant; *cf.* Rom. 1:18-21, Acts 14:16f., esp. Rom. 2:14f. Paul tends to put it somewhat in Stoic, natural-law language. I prefer John Baillie's way of stating the case, *The Idea of Revelation in Recent Thought,* New York, 1956, p. 13: "Such knowledge of God and of His laws as the heathen nations were observed to have was believed to be a relic of

salvation for the gentile through the Noachitic covenant is mediated exclusively through Scriptures. Finally, the conclusion from Maimonides' requirement is that all who derive their basic moral law from the Hebrew Bible, Christian as well as Moslem, are unmistakably encompassed by divine grace even before they have accepted—as Judaism believes they will eventually accept—the plenitude of God's law and truth. Thus, Maimonides' famous conclusion concerning both Christianity and Islam is in complete accord with his legal view[27]: "The teachings of the Nazarene and of the Ishmaelite (Mohammed) serve the divine purpose of preparing the way for the Messiah, who is sent to make the whole world perfect by worshipping God with one spirit; for they have spread the words of the Scriptures and the law of truth over the wide globe, and whatever of errors they adhere to they will turn toward the full truth at the arrival of the messianic time."[28]

The Jewish "ecumenical" and Scriptural position can, then, be briefly stated: Judaism expects the eventual, messianic unification of all mankind under the truth of the whole

---

this original [Adamite or Noachite] revelation. And this way of accounting for the knowledge of God which the gentiles possess—a knowledge which, however overlaid and corrupted, is still sufficiently present in their minds to leave them 'without excuse' (Rom. 1:21)—is really much more germane to St. Paul's thought as a whole than the doctrine of Stoic origin which also influenced his writing at the beginning of the Roman epistle.—A similar preference is evident among the writers of our own generation whose thought we have been concerned to review. . . . Human nature is now regarded rather as the product of long historical experience, and whatever in it is good is regarded as the result, reflected in such experience, of God's historical dealings with the soul of man. . . ."

[27]Maimonides, ch. 11:4,—in the unexpurgated editions!

[28]*Cf.* also his responsum no. 58: "The Christians believe and profess in common with us that the Bible is of divine origin and given through Moses, our teacher; they have it completely written down, though they frequently interpret it differently." *Cf.* also R. Yehudah HaLevy's famous statement to the same effect, *Kusari,* IV, 23, and F. Rosenzweig's exposition of it in *Stern der Erloesung,* book III, part II, last page. *Re* this, also my paper "Rosenzweig," on p. 44.

Torah (written and oral) and, indeed, exerts itself toward this end even now. This may be termed "eschatological ecumenism." Until that consummation, the Jew is expected to assume individual and collective responsibility to this Torah, while the non-Jew attains to the same salvation by obedience to the (Scriptural) Noachite commandments. This may be termed "interim ecumenism." Finally, Jew and Christian, with complete respect for one another as seekers of the truth and of the pleasure of God, may and should vie with and for one another, toward the end that God's will for them and for the rest of mankind, revealed in Scriptures primarily as well as elsewhere, may become ever clearer to each of them and to all of them.

TOWARD A COMMON BIBLE?

by
David Noel Freedman

Thanks to widespread and continuing discussion in the popular press and more scholarly publications, the "common Bible" has become in the eyes of many an important goal of the ecumenical movement. Let it be said at once that a common Bible is an entirely legitimate and worthy objective toward the achievement of which much progress has already been made; and there is excellent promise of further attainment along these lines. At the same time it is important to define the common Bible more carefully and to evaluate its significance more realistically than would appear to be the case from some of the extravagant claims made for this project.

The issue is at once simpler and more complex than appears from the usual presentation of the common Bible. The emphasis is naturally on the achievement of a common translation or version that would be acceptable to the major religious groups and to the public in general. While that is a central element of concern, it is by no means the whole of the problem. On the one hand, a satisfactory English rendering of the Bible poses no insuperable difficulties. The Revised Standard Version of the Bible, under general Protestant sponsorship (though not exclusively), has had wide acceptance and not only among Protestant churches. The Catholic Confraternity version and the new Jewish Publication Society edition, though not complete, are also renderings of high merit and wide appeal. What is important about them is the comparatively slight differences among them. There is a common body of scholarship behind these versions which guarantees an essentially common result, subject to the usual variations of style and nuance. Sometimes one will catch the sense

133

of the original more felicitiously, sometimes another. Similarly one may stray inadvertently from the true meaning or reproduce the original woodenly, while another may catch the real significance of the passage in a daring turn of phrase or vivid figure of speech. But so far as I have been able to determine, the differences are not theologically significant and do not reflect in any way the ancient cleavages between the different religious bodies. It would take no great effort to compile a common Bible from existing translations, one which could satisfy the ecclesiastical authorities as to its fidelity, and scholars as to its accuracy, whatever literary shortcomings might result from such a procedure. In fact such a project is well along the road to publication and should appear shortly.

On the other hand, the common Bible involves a good deal more than simply a usable common translation. There remains the question of a common canon (i.e., a common table of contents), a common text (i.e., a common original Bible), and a common understanding expressed in a common rendering and commentary, to say nothing of the implications of such an enterprise for a common faith and finally a common Church. It is only as a link in a long chain of cooperative interfaith projects that the common Bible makes serious sense today. Otherwise it is simply a useful makeshift, designed to serve in those situations where a sectarian Bible would not do, as in interfaith ceremonies or study-groups, or possibly in the public schools. As such it would have immediate relevance and applicability to certain local short-term situations but in the long run promises more than it could fulfill. It would be helpful and desirable as a symbol of ecumenical activity and progress, but it should be clearly connected with the other aspects of the common Bible suggested above.

Without cooperative pursuit and attainment of these related objectives a common translation alone cannot guarantee the reunion of the churches or protect their unity once achieved. It will reflect the growing unity of the churches and their willingness to be associated in joint endeavors of importance, rather than create or promote it—though the impetus of a common translation in general use may itself contribute to the success of the ecumenical movement. At the same time it should be remembered that a common Bible is no guarantee of ecclesiastical unity: witness the dismaying fragmentation of Protestantism in the centuries after the Reformation, the many separating branches of the Church all appealing to the same Scriptures and often to the same translation to justify their independence. In short the Bible can be, as it has been, a source of division as well as of unity, and a common Bible no less than the ones in use hitherto and in our time.

With these considerations in mind, let us turn to the broad question of a common Bible.

1. A Common Scholarship

Underlying the enthusiasm for and movement toward a common Bible is a vast body of scholarship which forms the necessary foundation for any project in this field. The community of scholars crosses all confessional lines and includes many who profess no particular religious beliefs. It is an international group of scholars who have pooled their knowledge and through vigorous argument and debate have refined methods and attained results far in advance of previous efforts. The archaeological revolution—now in its second century of spectacular activity in the Near East—has contributed substantially to the growth of a common scholarship of the Bible. While no scholar stands entirely free of his confessional commitment and/or his philosophical and emotional presuppositions, and bias of some sort, in greater or lesser degree, is present in all scholarly work in this field, such prejudices or tendencies are more easily identified and discounted in an ecumenical setting, and in the course of discussion conflicting biases (elements of *Tendenz*) tend to cancel out.

135

In the present state of world biblical scholarship, it is not possible to speak of specifically Protestant, Catholic, or Jewish positions with respect to the interpretation of biblical or background materials, though different and opposing positions may be represented by scholars of one or the other of these faiths. There is a bewildering variety of groupings for and against different hypotheses cutting across traditional lines, thus effectively dissociating biblical scholarship from age-old ecclesiastical direction or control.

While we cannot speak of a scholarly consensus, if we mean agreement on all major scholarly issues relating to the Bible and its Near Eastern background, to say nothing of minor points, we can point to common scholarly assumptions, axioms, methodology, and a common body of technical results: archaeological, linguistic, and historical. And the body of assured results, universally accepted by qualified scholars in every country and of every religious background, increases all the time.

2. A Common Text

The first task of scholarship in dealing with the common Bible is the determination of a common text as close to the original text as it is possible to get. This is a complex and painstaking enterprise involving many scholars and many years of effort. At present five great textual projects are under way, some just started, others well-advanced, none complete. The first is a new critical edition of the Hebrew Bible under the sponsorship of the Hebrew University in Jerusalem. It is designed to replace the inadequate Biblia Hebraica of Kittel, now in general scholarly use, and will be based on the famous Aleppo Codex of the Old Testament, the oldest and best complete text known. A greatly expanded critical apparatus will be appended to the text, providing the significant variant readings of Hebrew MSS including the

Dead Sea Scrolls, as well as of the major versions: Septuagint, Peshitta, Vulgate, etc. This project has only been started in the last few years and may not be finished for decades. Valuable preliminary studies have been published, and the text and at least partial apparatus should appear within a reasonable time.

Continuing with the Old Testament, there is the long-term Septuagint project now nearing completion. The work has been carried on in England and Germany under separate auspices and with some variation in publication procedure and format. The Cambridge Old Testament in Greek covers the Historical Books, while the Göttingen Septuagint has proceeded with the Prophets and Writings. The combined work, of which the Cambridge volume on Genesis appeared in 1906, has proved an invaluable source for the oldest and most important of the versions of the Hebrew Bible; but because of the length of the time involved, it is already in need of revision in the light of new discoveries and the refinement of text-critical methods. But then, projects of such magnitude and requiring so much time for preparation and publication must always be regarded as being in process and subject to continual review and revision.

Next we may mention the International New Testament Project, now some years in process. With headquarters at the University of Chicago, it has enlisted scholars all over the world in the task of preparing an eclectic text of the Greek New Testament and as nearly exhaustive a critical apparatus as is now possible. Preliminary drafts have been circulated and official publication of selected books of the New Testament is expected to commence in due course.

Finally there are two projects dealing with principal versions of the Bible (both Old and New Testaments) of lesser significance for the determination of the original text, but of importance in their own right. They are the new critical edition of the Vulgate being prepared and published by the Benedictine Order, and the International Peshitta Project under Dutch sponsorship but utilizing an international team of scholars.

International and interfaith scholarly cooperation in massive studies of this kind received its initial impetus from the Dead Sea Scroll discoveries. Several volumes have already appeared, with many more yet to come, under the auspices of an international team of Catholic and Protestant scholars. Other scrolls, chiefly from the first cave, have been published by scholars in America and Israel, thus providing additional variety to the interfaith mixture. Many of these scrolls are texts of Old Testament books and have generated a great deal of new interest in textual studies in the Hebrew Bible and thus provide ample justification for the Hebrew Bible project mentioned above. At the same time recent discoveries of New Testament MSS (among the Bodmer papyri) along with a wide sampling of non-canonical Christian gospels and related literature (i.e. the Chenoboskion or Nag Hammadi Coptic texts) have provided welcome data for the study of the text of the New Testament.

The magnitude of these enterprises has necessitated cooperation on a large scale, thus involving scholars of different faiths and backgrounds. The international, interfaith team, especially in textual studies, has come into favor and contributed notably to the ecumenical cause in providing a solid non-controversial foundation for further cooperative ventures in the investigation of the Bible. It should be noted that textual studies, competently and carefully handled, are the most easily undertaken in cooperative efforts across sectarian lines and least likely to stir dogmatic controversies. These undertakings, especially those of an interfaith character, have proved of great value as exercises in cooperative scholarship. And they have demonstrated that in such work there is a scholarship common to all three faiths and to no faith in particular. While details will take decades to work out, and in fact the process of text-definition will never end, it is already possible to speak of a common text, that is a text of the Bible, representing the consensus of scholars, which most closely approaches the original—recognizing that in places it is not possible to determine which of two readings is superior or more original, and that in others the text is hopelessly corrupt, and recovery or reconstruction of the original is not presently possible. Apart from these considerations, there is already in the process of formation a common scholarly Bible —in Hebrew, Aramaic, and Greek.

3. *A Common Meaning*

By this we understand not simply the rendering or translation of the original into another language, nor the formal commentary which sets forth the interpretation and significance of the text, but rather the determination of the sense of the passage which underlies both translation and interpretation. We have reference to the "plain meaning" which is the proper subject of scholarly investigation, that is, to recover so far as possible the meaning intended by the author, in the light of the contemporary setting and available data. Beyond this, scholarship in the scientific sense can hardly go; in fact this goal itself is not easily realized, and there remain many obscurities in the text, many gaps in our knowledge, and many opportunities for progress toward this relatively simple and clearly defined objective. When it comes to the "fuller sense," or secret and hidden meanings unknown to the author, or esoteric implications and significations revealed to later inspired interpreters, we acknowledge the validity of the matter as a subject for inquiry and description, but we can hardly expect scholars to discover such meanings or justify them by historico-grammatical exegesis. The problem of pneumatic interpretation actually arises at a different point in the discussion and will be treated there. The proper elucidation of the plain meaning often requires more than a word-for-word rendering, either an extensive paraphrase or ample annotation explaining the circumstances or obscure details only hinted at or assumed in the original. If the object is to place the contemporary reader in the situation of the original audience, then he must be supplied with all relevant data assumed to be in the possession of those directly addressed by the author. As with the common text, so here too a scholarly consensus has been shaping for many years and—aside from the intractability of the material—there are no obstacles to further progress toward the recovery of the meaning of the original, which will be the common possession of all those concerned with the Bible.

4. A Common Rendering

A translation is a device for making a literary work available to people who are at home in another language. It is inevitably inadequate to its purpose: to be faithful to the original, and to do justice to the translation language. Since knowledge of the former steadily improves, while at the same time the latter is changing, all translations are provisional and require constant revision. To recreate for the new audience the setting of the original and convey nuances and overtones along with the central core of meaning are generally beyond the skill of the translator or the capacity of the language, short of adding extensive notes and explanations, which would change the translation into a lengthy commentary and distort the impression of the original in other ways. In short, there is no easy solution to the problems of translation, as those who have attempted this arduous and thankless task have universally testified.

Under the circumstances the notion that a single certain translation can satisfy all the requirements of the original and serve the needs and purposes of the modern reader is unduly optimistic if not delusive. There is nothing wrong with a variety of translations, such as are available today, so long as they are reasonably faithful to the original and informed by a scientific scholarly spirit, rather than some frivolous or arbitrary intention. On the contrary, depending upon the particular concerns or objectives of the translator, there should be many translations of different kinds, each rendering a distinctive service to the reader: whether in formal or colloquial language, for public or private use; whether literal (word for word) or free (phrase for phrase, sense for sense), etc. Two points deserve special mention:

1. An official or exclusively authorized translation might be of questionable value, and could even become an obstacle to progress. Such a translation, approved by the major ecclesiastical bodies for use in churches (and synagogues) and at public functions, would serve an important purpose. It would also carry with it immense prestige and authority, and if of high scholarly and literary quality would surely dominate the English-speaking world. In time it might drive all competitors from the field, as in fact the King James Version did, over a period of centuries. Not only would translations, useful for private reading and valuable for unusual insights into the meaning of the original and rendering of the original into the translation tongue, be lost in this process, but the impulse for new translations might easily be inhibited, thus delaying or obstructing the normal process of revision and improvement. The better the official translation, the worse might be the effects in the long run.

Such dangers can be circumvented, of course, and the value of an authorized version should not be minimized. The churches need only stipulate the uses for which the translation is authorized, without prejudice to other translations in existence or yet to be made, which may be equally helpful or useful to the general reader. Further it should be officially recognized that the authorized translation is neither final nor perfect and a continuing committee of scholars should have as a permanent task the review and revision of the work—issuing new and improved editions at specified intervals until the time comes for a brand new translation.

The nature of the ecclesiastical endorsement is another consideration of importance. To approve a translation on doctrinal or dogmatic grounds or as otherwise conforming to ecclesiastical standards would imply, and only serve to perpetuate in the minds of many this notion, that the meaning and rendering of the Bible was somehow subject to the authority of church or synagogue. The authority of such bodies in matters of interpretation and application is a serious question in its own right. But the matter of rendering belongs in the realm of scholarship, and the only significant test is that of accuracy, whether the translator has done his work in accordance with the best available scientific data and methods: archaeological, historical, and linguistic. On the side of literary quality and acceptability, other criteria must be applied, but these too have nothing to do with doctrinal propriety. The worth of a translation depends finally upon its scholarly or literary excellence, which ecclesiastical authority cannot confer by approval, nor deny by disapproval. Scholarship must be free and responsible, but its responsibility is to be faithful to the text and meaning of the original.

2. In the pursuit of a common English Bible, we should nevertheless bear in mind that the only true common Bible is one that already exists, or once existed: the original text in the original languages, and then only insofar as it can be recovered by modern scholarship. A translation can at best imperfectly reflect the original. In the quest of an unattainable goal, therefore, the endeavor itself is often more important than the objective. Thus the work of translating, carried on by a suitable committee of scholars, chosen by the various ecclesiastical bodies, but including also eminent scholars without such affiliations, would provide a setting for cooperative

enterprise which would at once reflect and promote the ecumenical movement. Through such creative interchange and cross-fertilization of scholarly ideas, much more will be accomplished than a common translation; and the scholarly by-products of such activity may in the long run be more significan than the translation itself.

At the same time that such a committee is at work, other enterprises should be encouraged and undertaken. Formal committee translations are inevitably formal: slow and ponderous, suitable for solemn assemblies and public gatherings. But individual efforts at translation should also be spurred. What is needed is not one common Bible but many, which will reflect the diversity of meaning and variety of rendering possible in dealing with the Bible. It is said that the Bible suffers in translation more than any other great classic; this inescapable loss can be remedied in part at least by a multiplicity of renderings. In their variety and scope something of the range of the original can be captured. Often it is only through extensive trial and error that the most suitable expression is arrived at. We register a complaint about the existing and projected modern formal translations—e.g., the Revived Standard Version, the Confraternity, and the Jewish Public Society versions—because of their sectarian sponsorship. The translations themselves are unexceptionable in their scholarship and largely successful in the quality of their renderings, but they continue to bear the stamp of a particular ecclesiastical organization.

Surely the time has passed for such narrow sponsorship of an enterprise that is appropriately the task of all men of goodwill, and especially those who have been nurtured in the traditions of the Western world. The translations themselves hardly reflect the character of their sponsorship, and aside from minor and largely irrelevant details could each serve as the prototype of a general or common version. In short, the Bible and its translators are already ahead of the sponsoring organizations; it is to be hoped that future Bible translations will have the ecumenical backing and sponsorship they deserve.

5. *A Common Interpretation*

If the text of the Bible and its meaning can be determined satisfactorily, there should be no serious difficulty about a common interpretation. At this point the learned discussions among scholars of diverse backgrounds and beliefs have been helpful in locating and holding common ground. With respect to historical linguistic considerations, i.e., the explanation of the text in its local and temporal setting, the results of ecumenical scholarship are encouraging, and within the limits of reasonable scholarly disagreement, a common position is emerging. Certainly it cannot be said that scholarly positions are drawn along confessional lines or that usually divergences are greater between scholars of different faiths than among those of the same communion so far as interpretation and evaluation of biblical material are concerned. There is considerable ferment about critical questions, which is always a sign of vigor in any scholarly field, but the wide variety of views held by scholars cannot be grouped and labelled "Protestant," "Catholic," or "Jewish."

When we move from the realm of the strictly exegetical interpretation of the text to that of more esoteric and less scientific procedures, the situation becomes more complex. Since pneumatic exegesis has always been the special province of religious groups, and we would include here allegorical and typological exegesis, along with other less well known devices for interpreting the biblical text, it is naturally more difficult to deal with such matters in a dispassionate scholarly fashion. It is even less likely that scholarly analysis will ever alter or affect traditionally held interpretations of particular biblical passages, especially as these have been reinforced by the weight of opinion of the great doctors of Church and Synagogue. Nevertheless some progress has been made at least in classifying the different hermeneutical phenomena involved, and in analyzing the methods used and the results obtained. By drawing the boundaries between the areas of legitimate scientific inquiry and those which belong to tradition and faith, it is possible for ecumenical scholars to proceed together as far as those limits beyond which they must part company.

For the present it would seem preferable to describe the variety of "fuller meanings" objectively, indicating the different ways in which the Bible has been and can be interpreted beyond the plain meaning of the text, recognizing the flexibility, fluidity, and diversity of such approaches and treatments of the material. We would make a clear distinction between the recovery of the essential meanings of any passage and all those derived significations which can in any manner be drawn or developed from the text in the light of later Scripture or the experience of the religious community. To the latter we would attribute a derivative value so far as the original passage is concerned, but one of prime importance for the situation in which they arose and to which they were applied. In short, these derived meanings have a significant place in the history of those communities which preserved and cherished the Bible and found it meaningful in their continuing existence on earth.

Once it is recognized that the ongoing life of the Church and Synagogue was nourished by the Scriptures in their original or translated form and that all secondary meanings and interpretations, no matter how esoterically arrived at, are nevertheless derived from that original, then the renewed concern for the same original will be entirely understandable. For it is out of that original text that new meanings and applications will emerge to guide the life of the sacred people of God. Thus scholarly concern for the historical-linguistic exegesis of the original text may seem somewhat farfetched and remote from the current needs and demands of the reli-

145

gious community, but I am confident that such labors will provide the source materials upon which the Church and Synagogue may draw for inspiration and guidance, making the necessary adaptation and adjustment to the changing conditions of every new age.

I have confidence that the God of the Scriptures, who is also the Creator and Sustainer of Church and Synagogue, will not permit his words to perish or become outmoded, but will continually renew their meaning and force for the believing and worshipping community to which he has chosen to make known his history among men and his will for them. So long as the peoples of the Book agree as to the essential contents and their plain meaning, a freedom with respect to more esoteric patterns of interpretation and explanation may be granted.

6. *A Common Faith*

A common Bible should ultimately mean a common conviction and allegiance to a common God and lead to a reunion of the Church and the Synagogue, based on a common biblical faith. Such a consummation seems very far off indeed, but perhaps a distant vision is as necessary to progress as more practical schemes designed for immediate implementation. We picture the faith and order of the believing community growing out of its response to the summons of God in the Bible. Such words may have a familiar Protestant ring about them, but our intention and understanding are otherwise. The movement toward reunion is a dual one: backwards to the beginnings, the origin and roots of the community of faith, forwards to a common understanding and acceptance of the nuclear traditions of the past.

We think of the Bible here as the central expression and embodiment of the tradition of the people of God, as the key witness to the mighty deeds of the covenant Deity which form the foundation of all belief and provide the framework

146

for the organization and life of the divine community. Consequently the more accurate our knoweldge of that tradition and the more substantial our faith in and commitment to it, the closer we must draw to that original community of God and toward each other. That an open and honest reexamination of the sources of our faith will have serious repercussions in the established religious institutions and may undermine cherished notions about ancient doctrines and practices is a risk we must all be willing to take. That it can lead to a genuine renewal and reformation of the Church and Synagogue is also true, and more important.

7. A Common Canon

At the center of the discussion of the common Bible is the question of the canon or, put another way, that of Scripture and Tradition. There are groups in both the Protestant and Catholic camps who distinguish sharply between Scripture and Tradition, though they may differ seriously as to the relative value they place on each. It seems to me that there is a better approach to the matter, and one increasingly recognized by scholars: that there is a single stream to which both belong, not separate streams. Scripture itself is tradition, the product of the coalescence and reshaping of traditions. It arises out of and points to the tradition; it embodies many stages in the process by which the traditions of Israel and the early Church were solidified into fixed form. It is at the same time part of the endless process by which the sacred community expresses its self-consciousness as the people of God. Thus it takes the experiences which were determinative of its existence and normative for its way of life, shapes and interprets them, formulates and records them: a diary of its past history with God and a manual for its future conduct, i.e., the tradition by which it is to live. Scripture is the epitome of tradition, its first and finest flower. But there is a continuous

147

line from Scripture to Tradition, or from the Tradition formulated in Scripture and the tradition which finds expression in other ways. All belong to the experience and memory of the holy people and have their place because of it. Not all traditions are of equal merit; not all are true or important for the life of the community; and a constant process of careful sifting is the necessary characteristic of a self-critical reformable and reforming Church.

Scripture and Tradition, properly considered, blend together, with Scripture at the center from which traditions radiate outwards, or about which they collect. The key issue between Catholics and Protestants in the discussion of the canon is the Old Testament Apocrypha. They form a significant body of traditional material shedding invaluable light on the so-called intertestamental period (from the third to the first centuries B.C.). Quite apart from dogmatic considerations, the value of these books (and others like them from the same period, the so-called Pseudepigrapha) cannot be denied, especially by those who are seriously engaged in recovering the world of the Bible and its real meaning.

Perhaps the term deutero-canonical, suitably defined, could be revived and used for these books. For it would appear that while this literature is biblical in tone and character and belongs to the same tradition from which the (other) Old Testament books derive, it does not belong to the main stream of salvation history. In all likelihood the line of division should not be drawn precisely at this point, since other books of the Hebrew Bible might well be relegated to secondary status, like Esther or the Song of Songs. It might be well to consider various Jewish attempts to evaluate comparatively the different sections of the Hebrew Bible: the Torah was preeminent, with the Prophets, Former and Latter, not less the word of God, only slightly inferior in importance, while the Writings ranged widely from that status.

By thus graduating the contents of both Old and New

Testaments it would be possible to achieve a flexible and workable canon, inclusive and expandable, but recognizing significant distinctions in value and importance. Thus we can make place for ancient texts but newly come to light, as for example the Qumran scrolls which attest to a tradition within pre-Christian Judaism the nature and scope of which could not previously be estimated with accuracy. They are directly related to the story of faith and incidentally illuminate the subsequent history of Judaism and the origins of Christianity. By ready yet critical acceptance of tradition as decisive for the life of the Church and acknowledgement of Scripture at its center surrounded by traditional materials of great though lesser value, we may be able to do justice to this substantial issue. By combining Scripture and Tradition instead of opposing them, we will ultimately come to a better comprehension of both.

Properly understood, the quest for a common Bible involves the whole life of the believing community: sustained by a common scholarship we must proceed from a common text and a common understanding to a common rendering and a common interpretation. These will lead to a common faith expressed in a common canon, which in turn will provide the key to the pivotal question of Scripture and Tradition. In its resolution may well be the future of the ecumenical movement and the hope of ultimate reunion.

149

BIBLICAL THEOLOGY AND SCHOLASTIC THEOLOGY

by
Anthony A. Stephenson, S.J.

"Theologians all the world over," writes Father Sillem, "have embarked, under the guidance of the Holy Spirit, on the vast work of rethinking and reconstructing Christian theology as we have known it since the far-off days of the Counter-Reformation."[1] For this task the theologian needs elbow-room and the freedom to explore and reconnoitre. Since questions about theological method are among the hardest and most obscure among problems now being reconsidered, I emphasize at the outset that my contribution is exploratory and intended to stimulate, not terminate, discussion. For the solution of some of our problems must depend on a dialogue among theologians and on the collaboration of specialists in many different fields.

Theology is discourse about God : a reflective, coherent and systematic account of God and of his creatures, the world and man, in relation to him. A Christian theology is, primarily, such an account of the Christian *revelation:* a systematic account of the one true, living and transcendent God as in love and mercy he has entered into communication with man and revealed himself through his saving action in history.

How does theology differ from preaching and catechetics? In content the three activities are similar, but preaching is more directly concerned with the central kerygma and with evoking the response of faith and obedience, while theology is more theoretical and more complete ; it covers the whole field of revelation. Compared with catechetics, theology—and by

---

[1] E. A. Sillem, *Clergy Review,* July 1964, p. 447.

this word I shall henceforth mean Christian theology—is more
theoretical, more highly systematic and more intellectualist.
Theology is a science in a broad sense. Nevertheless, the best
theology will be a kneeling theology, never very far from
spirituality (piety) and worship. Theology, preaching and
catechizing shade into one another and may even be combined,
as they were in the pre-baptismal discourses of St. Cyril of
Jerusalem. Cyril's *Catecheses* are simultaneously the exposition of the Creed, the preaching of the Gospel, and (for he
described them as the imparting of a *gnosis*) theology.

My definition of (Christian) theology, it will be noticed
(and I recognize that some would challenge it as arbitrary or
even incorrect), limits its scope to the Hebrew-Christian
revelation and to the discussion of questions which arise fairly
directly out of that revelation and to which at least probable
answers can be derived from revelation. It includes the de-
fence of revelation: the commending of revelation as possible,
"reasonable" and good against the attacks of the heathen. It
excludes those doctrines of natural theology not contained in
revelation. This is not, of course, to ban the Christian theologian from being also a natural theologian or from entering
into dialogue with the philosophers and the scientists or from
constructing a synthesis of revelation and the rest of experience—indeed all these activities are legitimate and important
—but only to suggest that the distinction regularly drawn by
the classical theologians between revelation (which demands
divine faith) and reason should receive recognition in the
classification of theology. This terminological distinction
would incidentally have the practical advantage of facilitating
our (Catholic) dialogue with the Eastern Orthodox and the
Protestants, both of whom set some store by the distinction
and sometimes (with whatever justification) accuse the Latin
tradition of too insouciantly incorporating "Western cultural
accretions." Perhaps a distinction between "revealed theology" and "philosophical theology" would meet the situation

and show indisputably to all comers that Catholic theology knows what it is about when it (quite legitimately) attempts a synthesis of revealed and natural knowledge.

Theology, then, has for its "object" or subject-matter the Hebrew-Christian revelation. Where is this revelation to be found? It is obvious that at least the Creed and the central *massif* of Christian dogma is contained in the holy Scriptures, and for convenience—but without taking up a formal position on the subject or excluding the possibility that some secondary or peripheral doctrines may derive from apostolic tradition alone—I shall assume that the whole of revelation is contained in Scripture as read in, and according to the traditional mind of, the Church.

Theology, then, systematically expounds the divine Scriptures and especially the Gospel, which is the Good News of Jesus Christ. As Father Tavard has written: "The core of the revelation was not the teaching of a doctrine. It was the coming of a Presence among men." At this date it is perhaps not necessary to emphasize this, but since one still meets highly-educated Christians who assume that revelation takes the form of a set of abstract and general truths, so that a typical example of theological activity will be an elaborate discussion of the different kinds of grace, let us insist: centrally the Christian revelation is not the communication of a body of impersonal information; nor does it, centrally, consist of a collection of abstract truths. Rather, while Scripture contains the ten commandments, the Law, the Wisdom literature, the Prophets, the Sermon on the Mount, the parables, and much other lore and general teaching, yet centrally the revelation was God's self-disclosure and saving activity through a sacred history (*Heilsgeschichte*), that is, through providential, divine events and their inspired interpretation by the prophets and apostles. Even in the Old Testament the core is a series of events: the creation, the Fall, the call of Abraham and the election of Israel, the Exodus sequence of

153

events including the Covenant, the failure of Israel and the passing of its task to the remnant. In the New Testament it is still more evident that what is really central is the story of how God finally accomplished his merciful and redeeming purpose by the incarnation, death and resurrection of his Son, a story that culminated in the events of the Ascension, the sending of the Holy Spirit and the founding and commissioning of the Church. In its general shape, then, the biblical revelation is not to be compared to a philosophy. In its general shape it is less like a philosophical system, whether of Leibniz, Spinoza, Plato or Aristotle, than like some of the great secular stories: the *Aeneid,* for instance, the *Odyssey,* or the *Chanson de Roland.* Nor is it a mere coincidence that in two other famous epics, John Milton's *Paradise Lost* and *Paradise Regained,* the history of our redemption has been finely retold. The "Bible Histories" of our childhood tell the same story. In one respect Dante's *Divina Commedia* provides a better parallel to the Bible: insofar, that is, as both works are products of a distant and somewhat alien culture and a specialized erudition is necessary for their complete understanding. Yet to understand the central theme of the Bible very little special knowledge is necessary. In another respect the *Iliad* provides an analogy; for, though essentially narrative, the *Iliad* is immensely rich and contains much else besides its central story, so that it was regarded by the ancient Greeks as a great repository of traditional lore and wisdom.

If anyone doubts my contention that the biblical revelation takes the general form of a narrative of a particular sequence of events, I would refer him to the Apostles' Creed (and let him note the changes of tense, from past to present, to future) and to the speeches of Peter and Stephen in the first part of Acts.

But to say that revelation is not, ultimately, about propositions or general truths is not to say either that theology is not concerned with propositions or that it can dispense with

154

propositions. As a form of discourse, theology necessarily expresses itself through statements and propositions. Moreover, the direct and immediate object of theology is the biblical revelation which, through statements and propositions, records and interprets God's revealing and saving action in history.

There remains one further preliminary question, the question so admirably formulated and discussed by Father Johannes Beumer, S.J., in his book *Theologie als Glaubensverständnis.*[2] The question is this: what is the relation of theology to revelation? Does revelation provide theology with its premises or with its object (subject-matter)? If revelation simply provides theology with its premises, then theology's main task is to draw inferences, to use revelation as a springboard from which it launches itself towards the conquest of fresh territory. If, on the other hand, revelation is the object of theology, then the (main) task of theology is not necessarily to go beyond or outside it, but to contemplate, interpret and expound the revealed mysteries themselves.[3] Father Beumer has no doubt—and neither have I—that, primarily and essentially, revelation stands to theology not as premises but as object or subject-matter. Father Beumer, indeed, thinks that the contrasting view is irreconcilable with the teaching of Vatican I on the mysterious character of revelation and the respective functions of reason and faith.

To take this view is not to exclude speculation but it is to draw a fairly sharp line between speculation and theology proper. It is to insist that the place of speculation is subordinate and that the theologian's *first* duty is not to speculate about questions which revelation either does not answer or answers only obscurely, but to contemplate and expound the revelation's central and direct affirmations: *contemplata*

---

[2]Würzburg, 1953; see also Father Bernard Lonergan's valuable review-article in *Gregorianum*, 35 (1954), no. 4, pp. 630-48.
[3]I am not forgetting the distinction between *subjectum* and *objectum.*

tradere. It will be convenient to characterize this method of theology as apophatic and the alternative method as cataphatic. By an apophatic theology I shall mean not the theology or method of Denys the pseudo-Areopagite or of any other particular thinker, but simply a theology which recognizes and does scrupulous justice to the profoundly mysterious and transcendent character of revelation, to the inaccessible mystery of God's being and the sovereign freedom of his will—facts which underline the difficulties of speculation and the hazards of inference. By contrast we shall label as cataphatic any type of theology which takes the mysteriousness of the revealed mysteries less seriously and tends to be overconfident, in this sphere, about the powers of human reason.

I should explain that I am using the word "speculation" to denote not just any thinking of or about revelation—for any theology must do that—but a thinking "round and about" the revelation, a speculation that expends a high proportion of the theologian's energy in questions about the conditions or implications of the revelation or about unrevealed whys and hows of revealed facts.

But does not the exclusion of such speculation from the (primary and essential) task of theology greatly restrict the theologian's field and make the task of "the queen of the sciences" a paradoxically modest and humble one? Theology *is,* I believe, a modest and humble science. But its being the humble handmaid of the Word is the very condition of its queenly status. The intellectual activity required of the theologian is essentially secondary and derivative, not an original intellectual prowess. Like the literary critic, the theologian's task is primarily one of interpretation, of explanatory and appreciative exposition. Nor does this (completely traditional) conception of theology superannuate the theologian or make his task either trivial or one that can be completed in weeks or years or centuries. The analogy of Shakespearean criticism shows that. Literary criticism is explanatory and appreciative rather than creative and yet, though the mountain of Shakespearean criticism grows through the years and the centuries, its task is never done. Both to Shakespeare and to the Bible, Dryden's remark applies: "The last verse has not yet been sufficiently explicated."

The theologian, then, studies and expounds revelation in all its depth, subtlety and richness. The revealed data are not like the axioms and postulates of Euclid, whose point and purpose is to send us away from themselves to make further discoveries about space. They are more like a Paradise to which the Lord God has given man a key, inviting him to wander freely through its paths and to penetrate ever more deeply towards its secret and mysterious heart. The theologian first explores this Paradise himself, then introduces the uninitiated to it and provides him with a map. It is his task to comment on the fauna and flora of this strange world, to mark on the map its points of vantage and fair prospect, and discreetly and sensitively to characterize its beauties and delights. Like the gifted art-critic, the great theologian tells us where to look and what to look for, and opens our eyes to see more in what they see. Yes, art-criticism, and particularly the criticism of literature, the most intellectual of the arts, provides a better analogy than the beauties of nature. For while natural scenery delights, enchants and elevates, its meaning is elusive and the means employed largely defy analysis. The biblical revelation, by contrast, discloses depth beyond depth of intelligibility, even though this intelligibility is not the clarity of "clear and distinct ideas" and we can never pluck out the heart of its mystery. The interpretation of the Bible (which works largely through images) finds an analogy in the interpretation of a great play. We come to understand a Shakespearean tragedy insofar as we surrender ourselves to it, read and re-read it, seeking its principal and subordinate structures. Then the over-all pattern of thought and passion gradually produces its intended effect, and our response becomes more appropriate, integrated and precise. Gradually we gain insight into "the conduct of the plot," the delineation of character through speech and action, the versification and subtle orchestration of the imagery with its resembling, contrasting, ambivalent and neutral groups.

Looking at a picture provides another analogy. Here too progress in understanding comes through contemplation. The complex unity of a great painting is such that all the parts gain their significance from the whole and from one another; from every part of the canvas light is shed on every other part. There is only one way to grow in the understanding of any great work of visual art, and that is to look at it, and to go on looking. Then major and subordinate patterns gradually reveal themselves; new details and significances emerge, each enriching our understanding of the whole. This, I suggest, is rather the way in which we progress in the understanding of revelation.

But your own argument, it may be said, is beginning to progress rather erratically. You began by emphasizing that the central content of revelation is not a set of abstract philosophical propositions but a series of particular historical events, and now you are saying that one of the most illuminating analogies with the interpretation of the revelation is literary criticism—the appreciative elucidation of the *Iliad* or of *Hamlet*. But the techniques of Shakespearean critics like F. R. Leavis, Dover Wilson, Caroline Spurgeon or Wilson Knight do not seem at all appropriate to the study or interpretation of history: of, for example, the life of Gladstone or the history of England. When you speak of the detection of the central significance, of the intelligible structure and master-pattern of a work of art, we seem to be back at something much more like philosophy than history, which is composed of particulars and has much of the random, unintelligible and opaque character of bare fact. History is notably lacking in the pattern, intelligibility and design which can be discerned in *Hamlet.*

But first, while there is a relation of sheer contrast between the abstract universal and a concrete particular like a historical event, there is no such contrast between a particular event and certain "general" things like meaning or significance, quality and value—what the French, I think, call *la valeur.*[4] Secondly, while it is only too true that it is hard to find in secular history any very large historical sequence bearing the imprint of a grand design, this is clearly not true of sacred history (*Heilsgeschichte*). Here, on the contrary, we find one overmastering, persevering and irresistible design manifesting itself in a sequence of events that is at once unique and uniquely significant. It is, indeed possible so to expound the *Heilsgeschichte,* with such an exclusive emphasis on time and the particularity of historical events, that the resulting impression is like the view of a train from a hill top; the train is clearly enough travelling successfully from one point to another, but the visual image hardly suggests any precious freight, and the nearest it gets to evoking the terrors and splendors of Sinai is the puffs of smoke from the engine. No: all historical events have a density, a vertical dimension, a meaning, a richness; and this is eminently true of salvation history. Revelation is redemptive history culminating in that datable event wherein the Word became flesh. But it was *the Word* that became flesh, a Word full of grace and truth (reality?), and men were permitted to see that glory. In redemptive history the heavenly forms, the ideal values and patterns, receive concrete historical embodiment. This Jacob's Ladder quality belongs, in due measure and degree, to *all* the events of the *Heilsgeschichte;* they are all loaded with splendor, shining with significance, so that not all the inspired eloquence of the psalmists and the prophets can exhaust the

---

[4]I owe this interesting distinction to a conversation with Mr. Frankland, S.J., of the French Canadian province.

meaning and the promise of the Exodus sequence of events.

Three consequences follow. First, the door is opened to a philosophical interpretation of revelation, for philosophical thinking is clearly one way in which this kind of revelation can be explored. Nevertheless, to describe revelation itself as a "heavenly philosophy" is still misleading and it still remains to consider the appropriate rôle and techniques of philosophy in elucidating a revelation which is predominantly existential, interpersonal, "intersubjective" rather than metaphysical and primarily concerned with objects and natures. Secondly, because of the very richness of revelation, and because it is, in the pregnant theological sense, mysterious, and because it mediates a divine encounter, in man's response the accent must fall on faith, worship and contemplation rather than upon a limitless curiosity or a zeal for deduction and inference. Thirdly, the objection raised against the analogy with literary criticism disappears. Not that the biblical revelation is everywhere or even normally a work of literary art, but because the redemptive history which it records, though real and not fictitious history, is the expression of a grand design and consequently may well prove to exhibit the intelligibility and patterned structure which normally in the field of narrative are distinctive of creative writing and poetic invention.

Since certain streams of post-Tridentine and counter-Reformation theology are somewhat more cataphatic, some of the positions advocated here may seem revolutionary. To dispel any such notion, and to show that the apophatic approach goes back to an older and better tradition, let us glance at the principles of some earlier theologians. Systematic theology in the grand manner began with the third-century Alexandrian school. The rather ambitious (though quite legitimate) attempt of Clement and Origen to construct (apparently) a great synthesis of revealed and natural knowledge was probably encouraged by their belief that the Greek philosophers had borrowed their deepest insights from the Old

Testament. What I would here stress, however, is the highly apophatic principles of the Alexandrians. It was typical of Clement to declare that the Word is the sole teacher of *gnosis* (theology) and that "the whole *gnosis* from A to Z is contained in the Old and New Testaments."[5] It was no less characteristic of Origen to regard the construction of a Christian *gnosis* as essentially a task of biblical exegesis. We get some idea of the Alexandrian conception of theology from Origen's doctrine that enlightened faith (*gnosis*) differs from simple faith by the possession of the scriptural demonstration from miracles and prophecy.[6] Similarly Clement, while allowing that faith is *gnosis* after a fashion, a condensed or dehydrated (*suntomos*) *gnosis,* the genuine article is "a firm and solid demonstration of the truths received through (upon?) faith, being built upon faith through the Lord's teaching [the New Testament]."[7] Both Clement and Origen apparently regarded the task of theology as the conversion of simple faith into enlightened faith or *gnosis* by showing how "simple faith" derived from and was warranted by the revelation.

The same pattern reappears, with some important transpositions, in the *Catecheses* of Cyril of Jerusalem. In the Jerusalem pre-baptismal catechesis, the Creed was delivered to the candidates fairly early, and the syllabus of the catechetical lectures was the exposition and demonstration of the Creed from Scripture.[8] Like Clement and Origen, Cyril describes the provision of the "demonstration" of the Creed from Holy Writ as the imparting of a *gnosis*. Since Cyril describes the Creed as a compendium of the dogmatic content of Scripture—and in fact even *verbally* the Jerusalem Creed is at least 90% scriptural—the whole procedure may sound a little naive to ears accustomed to a more philosophical the-

---

[5]*Strom.*, VI, 7, 54 and 61 (*GCS*, XV, 459, 462) ; VII, 16, 95 (*GCS*, Clem. Alex., III, 67).
[6]*Contra Celsum*, I, 2 (*GCS*, Origenes, I, 57).
[7]*Strom.*, VII, 10, 57 (*GCS*, XVI, 42).
[8]*Cat.*, IV, 17; V, 12; XVIII, 22.

ology. Yet the position is exactly that maintained by St. Thomas in the *Summa* (I, q. 1, a. 8, *ad* 2) where he says that while human reason may throw light on some points of sacred doctrine, and the authority of doctors of the Church supplies a probable argument, yet the proper, and only compelling, argument in theology is the authority of sacred Scripture. Nor is Cyril's method really naive, though certainly its movement is "from faith to faith." Cyril's conversion of simple faith into knowledge or understanding (*gnosis*) by the scriptural "demonstration" had two functions. Besides "verifying" the articles of the creed which the candidates had received from the bishop,[9] it articulated the isolated credal propositions by relating them to their living context in revelation and the whole rich background of the *Heilsgeschichte*. It would, consequently, be of great interest to know whether Clement and Origen (for Cyril was not much of an original theorist) conceived of this theological method in conscious analogical dependence on Aristotle's conception of the "scientific demonstration" (the *apodeixis* in *episteme*) which confers intelligibility upon a truth and produces genuine knowledge by grounding the truth in explanatory first principles. Such a really "scientific" proof, showing not only that the fact is so but that it must be so, makes the original proposition luminous by deducing it from self-evident principles and by exhibiting it in its place in an articulated system of knowledge. In the proof from the word of God, which promotes simple faith into knowledge (or "understanding"?), there is both a contrast to epistemonic *apodeixis* (for the revelation is not logically self-evident, but obscure) and an analogy, since the word of God has even greater authority, and grounds truth even more securely, than self-evidence. In such an

---

[9]*Cat.*, IV, 17; V, 12. Since it is the Church which possesses and interprets the Bible, besides delivering it to the candidate, she "verifies" her doctrine from her own resources: a nice illustration of Fr Tavard's formula of the "coinherence" of Holy Writ and Holy Church. Cf. *Cat.*, XVIII, 23: the Catholic Church teaches catholic (universal) *gnosis*.

inquiry, however, it would be necessary to determine the function of the argument (stressed by Origen; see above) from miracles and prophecy; but the *Catechesses* at least seems to be conceived as predominantly a work of dogmatic theology in which this *prima facie* apologetical argument, though prominent, is relatively subordinate and incidental.

Whatever may be thought, from the logical or epistemological point of view, of Cyril's demonstration of the Creed from Scripture, psychologically and spiritually the effect could be far-reaching, even dramatic. Between the possession of the Creed with and without the demonstration from Scripture there would be all the difference between the mere reading of the "argument" of *Hamlet* and the seeing of the play after a profound study of the poetry. Certainly there is an important sense in which Cyril's scriptural demonstration makes the creed "intelligible." It replaces the bare bones of the Creed with a sublime and richly articulated revelation that has the authentic ring of truth, supplies the key to life, and mediates an encounter with the Savior. In Clement the Scriptures seem to be regarded as being, when studied in depth, in some sense and degree, self-authenticating; their content contributes to their authority.

"Credo ut intellegam": "faith should be but the prelude to understanding": the formula has become a slogan. But what does it mean? That we believe the Creed, or revelation, in order to understand something *else?* That to accept Christianity is to possess the key to life and the universe? That the next step after accepting revelation is to show that it is rational, even to prove it by deducing it from rational principles? But a supernatural revelation cannot be proved by a logical or scientific deduction (though the apologist can provide "evidences" for its truth); nor, it is agreed, can it be shown to be rational, at least in the narrow sense, though it can be defended and shown not to be irrational. Or that we should conceptualize the revelation by translating it, with the aid of ordinary and technical language, into the terms of the prevailing (or perennial) philosophy, and relate it to the whole of our experience? Certainly there is much to be said for this. Yet I wonder if this is really either the deep or the original meaning of the formula. Be that as it may, for Clement, Origen and Cyril, the movement of theology is "from faith to faith." They held that faith is not a *means* to anything except itself or what it begets or flowers in within its own order. For them faith *contrasts* with "understanding" or knowledge only in the sense of *gnosis,* the "enlightened faith" which comes from a longer exposure to the word of God, that powerful and sovereign word which, witnessing to the Word, both creates and enlightens saving faith and calls into existence a holy people. In the matter of speculation, of course, Cyril contrasts somewhat with the Alexandrians. Cyril disapproved of speculation and distrusted philosophy: "concerning God, it is high knowledge to confess our want of knowledge"; "in speaking of the divine and sacred mysteries of the faith we should avoid even any incidental remark that has not warrant of holy Scripture."[10] In the *Catechetical Lectures,* then, of this great Doctor of the Church we have a contemplative mind's systematic (in a very broad sense) exposition of the biblical revelation in its own terms. Though Cryil's tools and technique were imperfect, he has given us a notable pioneering work in biblical theology.

Scholastic Theology

Scholastic theology, if one is to define it in eight words, is the translation of the biblical revelation into Greek; that is, into the concepts and terminology of ancient Greek philosophy. In the Thomist tradition, to which I must confine myself, the terminology is predominantly Aristotelean. In substance and doctrine, scholastic theology is highly biblical; for theology is not the same thing as doctrine, and the same doc-

---

[10] IV, 17; VI, 2; cf. V, 12.

trines can be expressed in several different theologies. Scholastic theology, however, has the shape and uses the tools of a philosophy. It is characteristically somewhat speculative and, while highly analytic, interested in a synthesis of revealed and natural knowledge. It has a strong metaphysical bent and is interested in questions of being and natures. Its habits of analysis tend to a splintering of the revelation, so that one finds separate treatments of dogmatic, mystical, moral and pastoral theology, liturgy and spirituality (piety). It is less of a "kneeling theology" than biblical theology. Though implicitly or latently personal, evangelical and kerygmatic, formally and actually it is somewhat dry and abstract. Though never denying, indeed always implying, the personal character of revelation, it manages to give the impression that it is impersonal. For example, until Father Schillebeeckx recently gave us his splendid exposition of sacraments as encounters with the risen Christ, scholastic theology would devote much attention to the nature of sacramental causality and, after briefly recognizing that Christ is "the principal agent," would explore the secondary or instrumental causality of the sacramental rite. How well I remember my satisfaction with Cardinal Billot's conclusion, that sacramental causality is, if I remember correctly, an instrumental, dispositive, intentional, efficient causality!

Scholastic theology has been, on the whole, especially in its classical period, apophatic. Many scholars would say that the rise of the counter-Reformation movement introduced a less apophatic theology. I think on the whole that this is not true. Nevertheless one can perhaps detect three tendencies having cataphatic affinities. There was, first, the fairly general tendency to substitute a two-source theory (Scripture *and* apostolic tradition) of revelation for the one-source theory (Scripture as interpreted by tradition). Secondly, there was a minority tendency to hold that where a conclusion depends on one revealed and one unrevealed premise, the conclusion can yet be not merely certainly true but equivalently revealed and *de fide,* for the authority of the Church "converts" the conclusion into a truth having divine certainty. Thus it can be a truth *de fide divina* that the reigning Pope is truly a successor of St. Peter. A more apophatic theology would say that this truth, like the truths that "this Mass which I am attending is a valid Mass" and "this baby is certainly regenerate, because I am sure that I have validly baptized it" are morally, or even by reduction metaphysically, certain and have the further guarantee of divine providence. Thirdly, there was a gradual and slight *practical* change of emphasis, in the teaching of theology, from the ultimate criterion (the revelation) to the proximate criterion, the teaching of the Church. Where St. Cyril, for instance, began with credal and biblical propositions and "demonstrated" them from Scripture, the modern (or recent) theological manual often takes a thesis formulated in abstract conciliar language and then checks it against Scripture by the use of proof-texts. But these inconspicuous tendencies have been offset and controlled by an unwavering emphasis on the unique authority of revelation and on the unchanging identity of doctrine (regularly regarded as bound up with the indefectibility of the Church). I do, however, seem to detect the emergence of a definite cataphaticism in a certain stream of theology in the last hundred years; more accurately, since about 1845, the date of Newman's *Essay on the Development of Christian Doctrine,* in which work—originating, as I believe, a new conception of doctrinal development—the cataphatic spirit has found its most powerful, systematic and original expression[11] (though Newman is commonly elsewhere apophatic).

---

[11]In the paper written for Fr. Flanagan and elucidating the *Essay,* Newman speaks of (definable *de fide*) deductions and developments "indefinitely and without limit numerous." See C. S. Dessain, "An Unpublished Paper by Cardinal Newman on the Development of Doctrine," *Journal of Theological Studies,* N. S., IX (1958), 324-335; p. 329.

Some, whether applauding or deploring, would say that the adoption of the Aristotelean method and categories gave Scholasticism an inherent cataphatic bent almost from the start, and that St. Thomas himself essentially anticipated Newman's conception of doctrinal development. My impression is that the baptizing of Aristotle led to a tension within theology; in any case, the dangers arising from the philosophic spirit have been effectively averted by the magistracy in accordance with the fundamental theological principles mentioned above. The final answers, however, to questions about St. Thomas's and Newman's theological methods—and perhaps also about the true nature of a good apophaticism—must wait upon further discussion and clarification. In my view, however, scholastic theology, in spite of its interest in deduction and in the peripheral, has remained, essentially and on the whole, apophatic.

In its interest in an intellectual synthesis of a metaphysical kind, scholastic theology was perhaps continuing and developing a tendency of the third-century Alexandrian school; for their Christian *gnosis* was intended to overthrow and replace the false pagan *gnosis,* whose object was God, the self, and the cosmos.

Technical philosophical terminology entered Christian theological discussion at least as early as the third century, and the highly technical term "consubstantial" (*homoousios*) was canonized by Nicaea I. But scholasticism has fully arrived only when the full paraphernalia of Aristotle's logic, metaphysics, etc., is admitted to theology, and a systematic and fairly complete exposition of revelation is carried through in the concepts of Greek philosophy. In the heyday of scholaticism not only such terms as nature and hypostasis, but also the doctrines of matter and form, potency and act, substance and accident, the various kinds of cause, and a host of technical adverbs for use in distinctions are ubiquitous—and perform a useful function.

Since theology is the science of revelation, it is "the science of a Book," and it was so regarded and so very commonly styled, as Father M.-D. Chenu has pointed out, in the pre-scholastic and Early Mediaeval periods. Theology was mainly scriptural exegesis, and its tools and techniques were literary. After the discovery and translation of Aristotle's major works these literary tools were progressively superseded by dialectical and philosophical methods. Aristotle did not gain entry unchallenged. In England, Roger Bacon sounded the alarm. St. Bonaventure protested: "One is our Master, Christ." And Pope Gregory IX, in his letter *"Ab Aegyptiis"*[12] to the theologians of Paris in the year 1228, denounced in vehement terms those theologians who presumed to adulterate the "heavenly oracle" with the doctrines of philosophy. They will drink again, he said, of the living water only when they have sent this concubine (philosophy) packing and returned to their true Spouse, the word of God. A generation earlier Stephen of Tournai, the papal nuncio at Paris, had complained that owing to the revolution in theological method the Holy Trinity was being dissected and torn limb from limb at every street corner. Where previously the Bible had been the only text-book, it was now joined by the *Sentences* of Peter Lombard, and major theological works took the form of commentaries on the *Sentences* which also provided the framework for theological work in depth; upon it also, the *Magistri Sententiarii* lectured. Scriptural exegesis continued but seems to have yielded pride of place to the new method of "Questions" (the investigation of problems) and "Disputations." This more dialectical and speculative exercise now provided the growing-point in theology. This was the University period of theology, and in the intellectual ferment of the Renaissance theologians also felt the impulse to take all knowledge

---

[12]Reproduced in Denzinger, *Enchiridion Symbolorum,* etc. (ed. 31). Cf. n. 442. M.-D. Chenu, *La théologie comme science au xiiie siècle* (Paris, 1957), Chap. 1—an invaluable work on its historical side.

for their province and to attempt a mighty synthesis. Theologians were infected by the old, noble ideal of knowledge and causal explanation (*rerum cognoscere causas—primus Graius homo*).

Here we may notice two problems, without attempting a definitive solution. First, it is commonly said nowadays, and with much truth, whatever qualifications may be desirable, that there is a sharp contrast between Greek categories and thought-forms and the predominantly Hebrew categories of the biblical revelation. Fourth-century Greek philosophy is a static philosophy of essences, interested in general ideas and abstract definitions, while Hebrew thought is concrete and dynamic. In the Bible, time and history are of the essence, while for Plato reality and salvation are to be sought outside time, and even Aristotle ("poetry is more philosophical than history") has the descending gradation: philosophy, poetry, history. The "objective" Greek philosophy, again, seems not to be the best vehicle for interpreting the highly personalist and existential revelation, a revelation moreover given through particular events. It is, however, between Hebrew and Platonic thought-forms that the contrast is sharpest, and St. Thomas modified Aristotle's philosophy in the direction of the concrete real.

The second problem is this. In the Middle Ages—and possibly long before—Christian theologians sometimes read the Bible through Greek eyes. Even in quite modern times the mistranslation of Apoc. 10:6 as "Time shall be no more" instead of "There shall be no more delay" was perhaps due to the importance which the Platonic idea of eternity has gained in Christian thinking. Similarly it is at least very doubtful if Exodus 3:14 is correctly translated by the LXX's rendering, equivalent to "I am He who is," though this translation played an important part in St. Thomas' system. Similarly it is interesting to ask whether the somewhat impersonal scholastic concept of God as (sometimes) "an infinite sea of

169

Being" or as the *Actus Purus* or *esse subsistens* really derives from revelation and not rather from natural theology. The *Actus Purus* is conceived as utterly "simple" in the meta-physical sense, i.e., as excluding all multiplicity and real distinction of attributes. In God there is no succession of acts, whether of love, knowledge or decision. Again, the *Actus Purus* is eternal not only in the sense that he is from ever-lasting unto everlasting; not only in the sense that He is above astronomical time and transcends man's past, present and future, and is the Lord of time and of history; but he is also timeless in that sense of time in which time "prevents everything happening at once"; he does not remember or fore-see or plan; his decisions are eternal in the sense in which geometrical entities are eternal, though they take effect (*terminative*) at different moments of time. The Word was not changed or affected by the incarnation—except in the human nature which He assumed. This is not, of course, to question the truth of this conception—a biblical theologian is not likely to forget that God is "wholly Other" and likely to be different from what he might expect; at the least, more-over, there is a very venerable tradition behind the concep-tion. It is only to ask whether the conception is revealed and whether, supposing that the God of the philosophers and the savants in fact differs in some respects from the living God of Abraham, Isaac and Jacob—or, more accurately, supposing that not the whole of the philosophic conception is contained in the revelation—whether the Christian (and not exclusively the Latin Catholic) tradition has sometimes supposed that the conception was fully biblical, and, if so, whether this was under the influence of Greek ideas—going right back, perhaps, to Plato's description of the Form of the Good. This would not, of course, tell against the truth of the conception, but that truth would now derive not from revelation, nor from the fact of its having been read into revelation, but from natural reason as (perhaps later) employed in natural theology; and

170

the conclusions of natural theology can enjoy metaphysical certainty—even apart from the further authority that some of them enjoy as a result of the approval of the Church.

Supposing on the other hand, that the conception has been defined *de fide*—and it looks as if at least some of it has been —and is therefore contained in the revelation, then I list a number of logical possibilities. 1) St. Thomas's interpretation of Exodus 3:14 as defining God as pure subsistent Being is, after all, correct. This seems not very probable,[13] and I hear (I have not checked it) that the lastest New Testament scholarship does not favor the view that the relevant passages in St. John's Gospel provide positive support for the metaphysical exegesis of the passage. 2) This metaphysics of the divine nature emerges from a number of other biblical passages, especially when taken together. 3) The conception had been absorbed from Greek philosophy into Palestinian thinking before A.D. 100 and is taken for granted, even if not explicitly formulated, by the New Testament writers. It is significant that the New Testament writers so freely used the Greek Old Testament in preference to the Hebrew, and at Exodus 3:14 the LXX reads "I am He who is," *ego eimi ho on,* which has quite a Platonic ring. 4) The relevant propositions have been defined "secundum sensum Scripturae."

In the new (32nd) edition of Denzinger the "index systematicus," B1a and B1b, seems to show some awareness of the problem and to offer some guidance. The metaphysical definition of the divine essence as *esse subsistens* is qualified as "according to the Thomist school" and *aeternus* is glossed as *sempiternus* (everlasting). It is, however, the attribute of immutability that, when understood ontologically, yields an eternity of a Platonic type, and on the interpretation of this attribute no help is given.

It is often said that a great advantage of scholastic theology

---

[13]Albright, however, has advocated the translation, "He who causes to be."

is its precision. This is true, but the statement is itself somewhat imprecise. If what is meant is that scholastic formulas often hit off very exactly and happily a specific aspect of some revealed mystery, this is true. But insofar as the statement may suggest that scholastic formulas are uniquely qualified to hit off the *whole* of the relevant mystery—in the sense in which we say of a felicitous portrait that is "the living image" of its original—then it is arguable whether in *this* respect scholastic theology has the advantage over biblical. It may, however, be said that a full-blooded scholastic program could eventually cover the whole of the revelation, giving rigorous philosophical expression to every aspect of every revealed dogma and mystery, and so give a picture of the revelation that was both precise and complete. But one wonders whether the result of such a formidable program could altogether escape those dangers which ever threaten a philosophical theology, dryness and legalism. Abstract precision is won through analysis and dissection, and this may involve a high price: "we murder to dissect."

St. Thomas's Theological Method

Since, in spite of much recent valuable and enlightening discussion of this important question—all the more important because St. Thomas's theology has been largely normative for subsequent Catholic scholasticism—the subject has not been completely clarified, I shall confine my discussion to a few points, and here my conclusions will be tentative and provisional.

The main problem arises from the fact that St. Thomas adopted Aristotle's ideal of "science" (*episteme*), in some sense, as a model for theological method. Now, since science-*episteme* presupposes a highly rational conception of knowledge and envisages for its object a field of reality into which the intellect has clear insight and over which it has mastery, the question arises whether such a method, when applied in theology to the revealed mysteries, can be apophatic in the traditional sense. A theology modelled on *episteme* would seem to have an inherent drive to concentrate not on the revelation itself but rather on its unrevealed antecedent conditions and/or its implications and consequences. It looks like a theology preoccupied with theological conclusions instead of an exploration in depth of the revelation itself: predominantly speculation instead of contemplation.

Episteme is characteristically associated with a conceptualist and essentialist type of philosophy interested in species and genera and their differentiating properties and attributes. Aristotelian "science" was the expression of a rational philosophy seeking everywhere "evidence" in the philosophical sense: based on self-evident principles, working with luminous concepts, reasoning syllogistically and seeking to explain phenomena through their highest causes. *Episteme* can operate at full throttle only when this luminous quality is present in its concepts. It deals, moreover, in general propositions, for all its syllogisms are *in Barbara*.

There could, of course, be no question of a straight identification of revealed theology with *episteme,* but St. Thomas called Theology a "subalternate" form of it, i.e., that inferior form of science which, in Aristotle's system, does not have insight into its own first principles but borrows them from a superior science, takes them on faith and uses them. As optics, St. Thomas says, borrows its principles from geometry so the theologian receives his principles from revelation. Now, the "optician" can get on with his job without being a geometer, but a subalternate science, Aristotle was clear, is not genuinely science unless it can at need gain insight into the principles it borrows; and St. Thomas was pretty emphatic that theology is in some way a genuine "science" in the newly discovered Aristotelian sense.

The question has therefore been asked whether St. Thomas,

who in some places identifies the revealed articles with the "first principles" (self-evident in *episteme*), inaugurated a revolution in theological method, repudiated or modified the apophatic principles of twelve centuries, and was in fact a thoroughly cataphatic theologian who regarded theology as comparable to a highly abstract science like geometry in which from a few axioms and postulates a vast structure of knowledge is derived with rigorous logical necessity. The revealed mysteries would then be a sort of launching-pad from which the theologian would soar into metaphysical orbit, to return in due course to earth with elaborate chains of reasoning and spectacular theological conclusions.

I hope to show that such a conception of theology is very far from being St. Thomas's conception. Certainly such a conception would be as paradoxical as revolutionary. For the Christian theologian's data, so far from being a set of general propositions, or a system of abstract essences, consist, centrally, of a series of particular historical events. Moreover, the revealed mysteries, so far from being transparently clear, are notoriously "obscure" in the pregnant theological sense. It is for these reasons that St. Thomas's description of theology as a *scientia-episteme* has recently led some Catholic scholars to express some doubts about the truly apophatic character of this theology, and even to hint that his method was difficult to reconcile with Vatican I's classical statement of the traditional apophatic principle in the famous passage[14] demarcating the respective spheres of faith and reason, sharply contrasting the divine revelation with philosophical systems, and emphasizing (against Günther's *spekulative Idee*) that in respect to the revealed mysteries created reason can never have the sort of insight which it enjoys in its own realm. The supernatural mysteries, the Council insisted, transcend reason and remain for us in this life forever veiled in a dark mantle of mist.

---

[14]Denzinger (ed. 31), nos. 1795-1800.

One or two other recent interpreters of St. Thomas have maintained, on the other hand, that St. Thomas did regard theology as a *Scientia* in a "proper," not just loose and analogous, sense, but have sought to justify this conception, arguing that, since faith is a participation in the divine knowledge (the superior science whence theology gets its principles) and is in some sense continuous with the beatific vision in which it is destined eventually to flower, it does have the sort and degree of insight into the mysteries necessary to make *episteme* an appropriate method in theology and to justify the conception of theology as using the revelation as premises and as largely interested in conclusions. For my part, while recognizing that inference and deduction have their (subordinate) place in theology, I, like Father Beumer, find it impossible to reconcile any strong theory of this kind either with traditional Christian principles or with the teaching of Vatican I. Nor do I see much force in the supporting argument; the facts that faith is a participation in the divine knowledge and an anticipation of the beatific vision have always been recognized alongside the emphatic recognition that cognitionally faith contrasts with the divine knowledge as imperfect with perfect, and with the beatific vision precisely as unclear with clear: in fact, as faith with vision.

Father Lonergan accepts in general Father Beumer's conception of theology as essentially an *intellectus fidei* rather than as being largely concerned with implications and the advance into fresh territory. He holds, however, that St. Thomas illustrates Father Beumer's conception of theology and so confirms his general thesis. He shows, in some brilliant pages in the article already cited, that it is a mistake to suppose that *episteme* and syllogistic reasoning are necessarily or even primarily concerned with conclusions from data or with the discovery of new facts. On the contrary, the epistemonic syllogism is characteristically much less concerned with the discovery of new truths (and never with the discovery of particular facts or singular propositions) than with the generation of the understanding of the data themselves—the making of the factual data intelligible. So *scientia* is exactly what Father Beumer and all good apophatic theologians have been looking for! In the concept of *intellectus fidei* earlier theologians had had an admirable ideal of theology, but the implementation of the ideal had been somewhat vague and haphazard because the program had lacked a method. Now in *scientia-episteme* it had found the perfect tool.

Father Lonergan's article has thrown a great deal of light on the whole question. Nevertheless, although Albert the Great had pioneered the trail and the Alexandrian *gnosis* probably provided some sort of precedent, St. Thomas, I believe, inaugurated a new era and a new project in theology. His theology is not just a more methodical and scientific continuation of the pre-scholastic and early mediaeval theology, when theology was regarded as "the science of a Book" and as having for its subject-matter the redemptive history. It is significant that in answer to the objection that "science" is not concerned with singulars, whereas Scripture is, for example in the histories of Abraham, Isaac and Jacob (shades of Pascal!), St. Thomas replies (I, 1, 2, ad 2) that particular events in the Bible are not very important in themselves but are introduced "in exemplum vitae" or (cf. a. 10, *sed contra*) for their mystical significance. Moreover, St. Thomas proclaims a new project quite clearly in his definition of theology at the beginning of the *Summa:* "The subject of this science is God." When he takes for his subject God and, secondarily, creatures in relation to him, this is an announcement of a synthesis of revealed and natural knowledge, of revealed and natural theology whose central idea—for between finite and infinite the bridge is analogy—will be being: Being and being. Already in the thirteenth century the Renaissance thirst for knowledge was stirring, a revival of the Greek aspiration to know and to unify knowledge. St.

Thomas's *philosophical* interests were immensely strong. This strongly speculative interest and the nature of St. Thomas's project possibly partially explain that baffling phenomenon, the fact that one can collect from St. Thomas's works an impressive anthology of highly apophatic statements of method and principles and an equally long *catena* of apparently cataphatic statements. This fact becomes less surprising when we remember that St. Thomas's project included both dogmatic theology and natural theology, which is a branch of philosophy, so that he would be sometimes thinking in terms of the one and sometimes of the other. St. Thomas was engaged in the immensely important task—as urgent in our own day as it was in his—of the dialogue with the philosophers, the savants, the devotees of other religions, and agnostics. He was right in his profound insight that all knowledge does form, in some sense, a unity. But this task is also immensely difficult, so we can now add four further notes to our characterization of scholastic theology. It is contemplative *and* speculative. It is more interested in, and better equipped for, the dialogue with non-Christians than is biblical theology. And it is a very difficult, advanced kind of theology; it belongs to a high, even post-graduate, academic level. I am tempted to say, except that the word may seem disrespectful (though for me it is a term of the highest respect), that it is a theology for boffins: for those rare few who have a talent for philosophy and for constructive, or at least appreciative, thinking at the farthest frontiers. As a pastoral theology to be handed on to the people, biblical theology has the advantage.

But must we not class as cataphatic a theology which synthesizes revealed and natural knowledge and speculates largely about the revelation and its implications? Not necessarily. On account of the special concerns of the liberal theologian today—apt to want a recovery of primitive emphases and to prefer biblical to philosophical formulas—there is

177

a danger of our judging scholasticism's springtime by its later development, and so getting the whole thing upside down. For in St. Thomas there was a rebirth of the free Greek spirit in the service of the Hebrew revelation. He was a progressive and a liberal in his day, concerned negatively perhaps with the tyranny of a certain biblicism, and positively with the relation of revelation to all experience. If St. Thomas's metaphysical emphasis was conditioned by his time and interests, yet we must recognize that it is an important, though secondary, part of the theologian's task to consider the implications of the Gospel in such (additional) fields as sociology, economics, politics and psychology—even though revelation dictates little more than the spirit and the ultimate goals. But however ambitious a theological structure may be, it is cataphatic only if the theologian presents what is of its nature an amalgam as being all of a piece: if, that is, he claims the same divine authority for human thinking, however probable or certain it may be, as for the revealed elements.

There is no reason, I believe, to suppose that St. Thomas made this mistake, while there is every reason to suppose the contrary. For first, Aristotle himself, (though here I speak as one less wise) must surely have realized that unless his method could be modified, it could be applicable to no subject except pure mathematics. Indeed it is doubtfully applicable there, for has not Lord Russell said of mathematics that "it is the science in which no one knows what he is talking about, or whether what he says is true"? Aristotle, with his strong empirical interests (at least in his maturity) would have been forced either to recognize that his ideal science provided no sort of model or guidance for the investigation of the real world or to abate something of the rigor of his method and then apply it to reasoning where, according to the subject-matter and the particular circumstances, it would produce either certainty or varying degrees of probability.

178

That St. Thomas, in any case, drew some such kind of distinction between revealed truth, rational certainty, and more or less certain speculations based on *argumenta convenientiae,* is certain. Moreover, while his *prima facie* cataphatic statements are perfectly consistent with this hypothesis, especially in the light of the great diversity of his interests and the heterogeneous nature of his theological project, the series of assertions of apophatic principles is quite incompatible with the alternative hypothesis, that he had a cataphatic approach to "revealed theology." The former hypothesis explains both series of statements, the second only one.

That in the field of dogmatic ("revealed") theology St. Thomas was as apophatic a theologian as anyone could wish, seems abundantly clear from his very numerous apophatic statements, of which Father Paul de Vooght, O.S.B., has collected an interesting sample in a recent number of *Istina.*[15] To cite some of these examples: in his discussion of the Double Procession of the Holy Spirit (the *Filioque*) in the *Summa,* St. Thomas says: "We must say nothing about God except what is contained in Holy Scripture, either expressly or equivalently."[16] Thomas held that the Apostles had a profounder understanding of the incarnation than did the Christians of later ages.[17] He often justifies the use in theology of such non-scriptural words as person, essence, consubstantial, by saying that, though not the word, yet what the word signifies is taught by Scripture, and that any such novelties of expression are only new ways of expressing the same ancient faith.[18] He distinguishes sharply between the revelation made to the prophets and apostles (i.e., the Old Testament and New Testament) and any private revelation perhaps made to

---

[15]*"Le rapport écriture-tradition d'après S. Thomas & c," Istina,* 1961-62, no. 4, pp. 498-510.
[16]"Vel per verba vel per sensum": *Sum. theol.,* I, q. 36, a. 2, ad 1.
[17]*Sum. theol.* II-II, q. 174, a. 6.
[18]*Sum. theol.,* I, q. 29, a. 3, ad 1; III, q. 60, a. 8, ad 1; I, q. 39, a. 2, ad 2.

other teachers.[19] "We believe," he says again, "the prophets and apostles . . . but their successors we believe not save insofar as (*quantum*) they declare to us what those others left in writing."[20] He adopts St. Jerome's saying that those traditions which come to us without the authority of Scripture may be rejected as easily as they were first admitted.[21] Such quotations could be multiplied, but they were, of course, no more than the theological commonplaces of St. Thomas' as of earlier ages.

But if St. Thomas was definitely a "one-source man," one must add—lest the unsuspecting reader conclude that he was a "biblicist" and taught a *Scriptura sola* doctrine of a Protestant stamp—that he was also a strong papalist and that the above series of texts could be matched by an equally impressive list of assertions that it is the Church that is the authoritative interpreter of Scripture. What interests us here, however, is, first, that such texts as the above appear to prove decisively that in his approach to dogmatic theology St. Thomas was strongly apophatic, and, secondly, that what the *prima facie* cataphatic texts really show is that neither was he a biblicist in the other sense of wishing to declare a total severance between revealed and natural truth and so of relegating Christian revelation and experience to something like a private world. The position, I believe, of certain biblical theologians who defend this latter view is becoming increasingly difficult. St. Thomas saw that there must be some kind of unity in the whole of truth and he made an unsurpassed contribution towards solving the very difficult problem of that unification.[22]

---

[19]*Sum. theol.*, I, q. 1, a. 8, ad 2.
[20]*De Ver.*, q. 14, a. 10, ad 11.
[21]*Catena aurea in Matth.*, c. 13, n. 11; cf. Jerome, *Com. in evang. Matthaei*, '1'. 4, c. 23, v. 35-36 (PL, XXVI, 180).
[22]For this and other questions see two valuable articles by C. Dumont, S.J., "La refléxion sur la méthode théologique," *Nouv. rev. théol.*, 83 (1961) 1034-50 and 84 (1962) 17-35.

Biblical Theology

I have left myself little space for discussing biblical theology. I hope, however, that some sketch of it has already begun to take shape. And fortunately the essence of biblical theology can be stated in a few sentences. Biblical theology refrains from translating the revelation into Greek (Aristotle). Rather, it presents the revelation in its own terms. This means, since the language of the Bible is more personal and existential than the language of philosophy, that biblical theology has these qualities in a higher degree than scholastic theology; it is closer to worship and to spirituality. It provides magnificent material for preaching. It is contemplative, and its contemplation, like the *theoria* of the Fathers, is warmer, closer to encounter and adoration, than is the philosophical contemplation of scholastic theology. Though it is, like scholasticism, a dogmatic and systematic theology, it rarely takes its eye off the *Heilsgeschichte* or forgets that it is concerned not with essences and natures but with concrete historical events. It is apt to concentrate on the central—the great themes like creation, covenant, redemption, the Creed, the *Heilsgeschichte* and the mysteries of Father, Son and Holy Spirit, where scholasticism is sometimes tempted to pay disproportionate attention to some obscure and peripheral point just because its obscurity presents an intellectual challenge. This is one reason why biblical theology has the further attribute of being ecumenical; for it emphasizes the great central area of dogma which Catholics and Protestants hold in common. The continuing development of a flourishing Catholic biblical theology is ecumenically important also because then Catholics and Protestants (who lack a strong scholastic tradition) will be expressing their respective faiths in the same language, and the wide area of real agreement will become apparent, whereas when they use different languages they can easily seem, even within the area of agreement, to be expounding substantially different doctrines. We can then more fruitfully embark on a dialogue about points of real disagreement. The Biblical theology may also contribute to the ecumenical dialogue with non-Christians; it is perhaps to Dodd and Father J. L. McKenzie, S.J., (heirs here of St. Thomas and certain Fathers?) that we owe the insight that the Bible derives its authority partially from its intelligible content ("in the last resort a man can only believe what is believable and indeed compels belief"—though this was said by someone else). Another attribute, indeed essential property, of biblical theology is that its method and tools are literary; it prefers to work, not with abstract (I know that tricky epithet requires careful definition) concepts, but with the concrete, rich and dynamic biblical images. But biblical and scholastic theology overlap, and none of these contrasts and distinctions should be pressed too far.

Vatican I, I believe, in the chapter already cited, both gave Catholic biblical theology its modern charter and also described its central method in a fine and profound phrase. After stating that the transcendence of the revelation does not, naturally, prevent Christians from having some understanding—a truly fruitful understanding—of it, the Council taught that this understanding may be gained in two ways: "from the analogy of the things known in ordinary experience and from the connection of the mysteries with one another and with man's last end." Now, the method of analogy is central in *scholastic* theology, and notably in Thomism: the revealed mysteries are explored and expounded through the development of analogy of such natural concepts as those of person, being, nature, cause. The second method, though it has sometimes been understood as a further description of scholastic methodology, seems more meaningful if understood as a description of a central method in biblical theology. For biblical theology regards the revelation somewhat as a vast tapestry, richly colored and of unsurpassed beauty. The biblical theol-

182

ogian directs attention to the great, recurring themes and images such as light, salvation, water, election, covenant, which, like brilliant threads in a tapestry or the repeated forms and balanced masses in a painting, run through the Old and New Testaments, link together various incidents of the salvation history and bind them into a rich and complex unity.

Thus, after the example of the Fathers, the biblical theologian may take such a simple image as that of water and fruitfully link the primaeval waters of Genesis I (typifying both chaos and the womb of life), the destroying waters of the Deluge, the waters of the Red Sea which overwhelmed the Egyptians but saved the Israelites, the water drawn by Moses from the rock, the living water promised by Christ, and the life-giving waters of the baptismal re-birth and re-creation. The figure-reality, type-fulfilment relation between the two Testaments adds a dimension not to be found in an ordinary painting. Such a detection of patterns and cross-references can be immensely enlightening. The baptism and Passion of Jesus, for instance, throw light upon each other. For by enrolling himself among sinners and taking on himself, as the Lamb, the sins of the world, Christ dedicated himself to obedience and, in effect, to death. The voice from heaven establishes a link with the Suffering Servant in Deutero-Isaiah, and in the Passion we see the destiny of the Servant fulfilled and the mission of the Lamb accomplished. Both mysteries throw light on our baptism, in which we are consecrated to obedience and baptised into Christ's death and risen life. The Bible itself, moreover, illuminates its mysteries in terms of one another. The accounts of the Transfiguration, for instance, consciously link the two Testaments, show Jesus as the fulfilment of the Law and the Prophets, and throw light forward on the Passion, in the Greek called an Exodus, by which Jesus, the new Moses, liberates his people.

The transfiguration itself is linked by elaborate theological symbolism with the revelation to Moses on Sinai in Exodus 24—for example, the "after six days," the overshadowing cloud, the Voice from the cloud. Similarly the miraculous feeding of the five thousand in "a desert place" recalls the earlier manna in the wilderness, while Jesus' actions—taking the bread, looking up to heaven, giving thanks or saying the blessing (Mk. 6:41 *eulogēsen;* 14:22 *eulogēsas—eucharistēsas* in 14:23) and finally breaking the bread—clearly link the miracle with the institution of the Eucharist. The sudden manifestation of power and the lavish superabundance relate the incident to the eschatological banquet and so indicate that with Jesus' coming the Messianic Kingdom of the last Days has dawned, even though it has not yet fully arrived or been revealed; and of that Banquet the Eucharist is a pledge and foretaste. Thus in a way that appeals not so much to the abstract intellect as to the imagination, the senses, emotions and the whole personality, the episodes of the *Heilsgeschichte* illuminate one another; as their converging rays meet and mingle the result is something like an explosion of light and glory. This *shekinah*-quality is only partly the effect of the resulting clarification of the mysteries, it also results from the sense of concrete immediacy produced when the mysteries are seen not in their individual isolation but as interrelated and as somehow implying and including one another. Then the revelation *as a whole* comes alive and imposes itself upon us; the Gospel is transfigured; the *Heilsgeschichte* manifests its *geschichtlich* qualities: which means not that the events of Salvation History are *literally* re-presented or made present —this unbiblical and un-Thomist exaggeration should be avoided—but that they are in every generation relevant, "actual" (*actuel*), present in their saving power, guarantees and witnesses of the new wonders of grace which the Holy Spirit is ever working in the New Age.

The method is literary. So the literary critic explores (the example is singularly inappropriate) *Macbeth.* Not even

Shakespeare could realize for us the dread and horror of the central deed by one description; instead, he must evoke it for us by the haunting, recurrent theme of the dagger, by rumors of the convulsions of nature, by the commotion which the mere thought of regicide produces in "my single state of man," as well as by contrasting images of water and the perfumes of Arabia. So not even the inspired writers can paint for us the work of the Redemption by a description of the bare deed. Instead they describe it for us (among a great variety of images) as a new creation and a second Exodus, so that the whole Bible (I exaggerate) conspires to portray the great event towards which it moves. For even in Genesis I, as Von Rad has remarked, the Creator is the living God, the God of Israel, and in the very idea of *him* is already implicit the possibility of a New Creation. As John Donne observed (and the sermons of Lancelot Andrewes also, we should remember, mark a milestone in biblical theology), "He who brought light, not out of a lesser light, but out of darkness," he in a twinkling "can turn your darkness . . . into daylight." Similarly, Von Rad suggests, while in the opposing chaos and darkness we may see some hint of the mighty effort and cost of the Redemption, yet God's majestic power, creating by a word, suggests a complementary aspect of the New Creation whose birth will be without birth-pangs, so unexpected and swift will it be. Thus the account of the creation in Genesis anticipates and illuminates Deutero-Isaiah and Jeremiah, even as they in their turn look both forward to the New Covenant, the new name, the new song and the holy city of the New Jerusalem, and also backward, comforting Israel with the thought that it is the omnipotent creator who is concerned for man. Isaiah links together the Exodus, the Covenant and creation and deduces the promise of even mightier works of grace: " 'I am the Lord, your Holy One, the Creator of Israel, your King.' Thus says the Lord, who

185

makes a way in the sea . . . 'Behold I am doing a new thing.' "[23]

It is characteristic of the biblical theologian, then—and Oscar Cullmann is a fine example of the type—both to explore the individual words and ideas of the revelation (as Père Audet's study of *eucharistein* has illuminated the Eucharist) and to expound the revelation in its own terms and by cross-references within the Bible. Here again he resembles the literary critic, who is apt to say that "the meaning of the poem is the poem" and that something is lost in a prose paraphrase. Yet if great poetry is untranslatable, the Bible is not. But do not the very distinctiveness and individuality of the biblical idiom, its antiquity and remoteness, suggest that, to become meaningful to our generation or to any particular time or culture, it must be translated into the language and ideas of the prevailing philosophy? This would probably be true if the language of the Bible were philosophical, but in fact it seems to be a largely pre-philosophical language which in some mysterious way—possibly archetypal images are relevant—speaks directly to the mind and heart of every man.

---

[23]Isa. 43: 15, 16, 19.

ABOUT THE AUTHORS

Albert C. Outler, Methodist

Education:

Wofford College, B.A., 1928.
Emory University, B.D., 1933.
Yale University, Ph.D., 1938.

Publications:

"The Patristic Christian Ethos and Democracy," in *Science, Philosophy and Religion—Second Symposium.* New York, 1942.

"The Reformation and Classical Protestantism," *The Vitality of the Christian Tradition.* New York, 1944.

Psychotherapy and the Christian Message. New York, 1954.

St. Augustine: Confessions and Enchiridion, vol. VII in The Library of Christian Classics. Philadelphia, 1955.

"The Doctrine of the Person and Work of Jesus Christ in St. Augustine," *A Companion to the Study of St. Augustine.* New York, 1955.

"Some Concepts of Human Rights and Obligations in Classical Protestantism," *Natural Law and Natural Rights.* Dallas, The Southern Methodist University Press, 1957.

The Christian Tradition and the Unity We Seek. New York, 1957.

"Freud and the Domestication of Tragedy," *The Tragic Vision and the Christian Faith.* New York, 1957. Ch. 10.

"Our Common History as Christians," *The Nature of the Unity We Seek.* St. Louis, 1958.

"The Unity We Have," *Christian Unity in North America.* St. Louis, 1958. Ch. 6.

"The Ordeal of a General Practitioner," *How My Mind Has Changed*. Cleveland, 1961.

"The Renewal of the Christian Tradition," *Faith and Order Findings*. London, 1963.

John Wesley, New York, 1964.

Other Pertinent Information:

Pastor, Methodist Churches in the South Georgia Conference, 1928–37.

Professor, Duke University, 1938–45.

Professor, Yale University, 1945–51.

Professor, Southern Methodist University, 1951– .

Professor, Union Theological Seminary (summer terms, '43, '53.

Visiting Fellow, The Council of the Humanities, Princeton University, 1956–57.

Chairman, the Graduate Council of the Humanities, Southern Methodist University, 1960–63.

Methodist Delegate to the Third World Conference on Faith and Order, Lund, Sweden, 1952.

Member of Faith and Order Commission and Member of the Working Committee of the Faith and Order Commission, 1952– .

Chairman, North American Section of FOC Theological Study Commission on Tradition and Traditions, 1953–63.

Delegate, North American Conference on Faith and Order, Oberlin, 1957.

Member, Methodist Commission on Ecumenical Consultation, 1958– .

Delegate, the Third Assembly of the World Council of Churches, New Delhi, 1961.

Delegate (and vice-chairman), the Fourth World Conference on Faith and Order, Montreal, 1963.

Delegate, the General Conference of the Methodist Church, 1960 and 1964.

About the Authors

Robert McAfee Brown, Presbyterian

Education:

Amherst College, B.A. 1943, honorary D.D. 1958.
Union Theological Seminary, B.D. 1945.
Fulbright Grant to Mansfield College, Oxford, 1949–50.
Columbia University, Ph.D. 1951.

Publications:

P. T. Forsyth: Prophet for Today. Philadelphia, 1953.
The Spirit of Protestantism. New York, 1961.
An American Dialogue, co-author. New York, 1960.
Observer in Rome. New York, 1964.

Other Pertinent Information:

Dr. Brown served as professor of religion at Macalester College from 1951–53. Then from 1953–62 he was professor of theology at Union Theological Seminary, since when he is filling the position of professor of religion and theology in the Special Programs in Humanities at Stanford University. In 1959 Prof. Brown received an American Association of Theology Scholars fellowship grant. He participated in Vatican II as a protestant observer, and is presently an associate editor of the *Journal of Ecumenical Studies.*

John Meyendorff, Orthodox

Educational Background:

University of Paris (Sorbonne).
Orthodox Theological Institute of Paris.
B.Ph., B.D., Licencie es-Lettres (Paris).
Diplome de l'Ecole pratique des Hautes Etudes (Sorbonne).
Docteur es-Lettres (Paris).

189

Publications:

St. Gregoire Palamas et la mystique orthodoxe, Paris, Les Editions du Seuil, 1959.

Gregoire Palamas—Defense des saints hesychastes (critical Greek text, translation and commentary), 2 vol., Spicilegium Sacrum Lovaniense, 30–31, Louvain, 1959.

A Study on Gregory Palamas, London, Faith Press, 1964.

The Orthodox Church, Pantheon, New York, 1963. (French edition, Paris, 1960; Italian, 1961; German, 1962.)

Other Pertinent Information:

Father John Meyendorff has been successively lecturer and Assistant Professor of Church History in the Orthodox Theological Institute of Paris and accomplished research work in the field of Byzantine studies under the auspices of the "Centre National de la Recherche Scientifique." Presently he is Professor of Church History and Patristics at St. Vladimir's Orthodox Theological Seminary, Crestwood-Tuckahoe, New York, and is Lecturer in Byzantine Theology at the Harvard University, Dumbarton Oaks Research Library and Collection, and Adjunct Professor in the Department of Religion at Columbia University.

Since 1955 Father Meyendorff has held the position of president of "Syndesmes," an International Association of Orthodox Youth Movements. Previous to becoming a member of the Faith and Order Commission of the World Council of Churches, he was Vice-Chairman of the Youth Department of that organization.

Father Meyendorff's field of special research is Byzantine Spirituality and Ecclesiology.

About the Authors

George H. Tavard, Roman Catholic

Educational Background:

Ph.D., Seminary of Nancy.
S.T.D., University of Lyons.

Publications:

"Some Remarks on Liturgy as Tradition," *Worship,* Oct., 1954.
The Catholic Approach to Protestantism. New York, 1955.
Protestantism. New York, 1959.
Holy Writ or Holy Church. New York, 1959.
Two Centuries of Ecumenism. South Bend, Ind., 1960.
"Tradition and Scripture," *Union Seminary Quarterly,* May, 1961.
"Authority of Scripture and Tradition," in *Problems of Authority.* Baltimore, 1962.
The Quest for Catholicity, New York, 1964.

Other Pertinent Information:

Father Tavard was formerly Professor of Theology at Surrey, England, and a member of the faculty at Assumption College, Worcester, Massachusetts. Presently, he is Chairman of the Department of Theology, Mount Mercy College, a member of the 25-man Secretariat for the Unity of Christians, a *peritus* at Vatican II and an associate editor of the *Journal of Ecumenical Studies.*

Markus Barth, Presbyterian

Educational Background:

Berne, Switzerland, 1934–35.
Basel, Switzerland, 1935–37.
Berlin, Germany, 1937.
Edinburgh, Scotland, 1938–39.

Doctorate of Theology, University of Goettingen, Germany, 1947, in the field of New Testament.

Publications:

Das Abendmahl, Passamahl, Bundesmahl, und Messiasmahl. Zurich, 1945.

Der Augenzeuge, Eine Untersuchung ueber die Wahrnehmung des Menschensohnes durch die Apostel. Zurich, 1946.

Die Taufe—ein Sakrament? ein exegetischer Beitrag. Zurich, 1951.

The Broken Wall, A Study in Ephesians. Philadelphia, 1959.

Was Christ's Death a Sacrifice? Edinburgh, 1961.

Acquittal by Resurrection (V. Fletcher, co-author). New York, 1963.

Sermons, articles, and reviews in Journals.

Other Pertinent Information:

After being the Parish minister of the Evangelical Reformed Church in Bubendorf, Basselland (Switzerland) from 1940–53, Professor Barth became visiting professor of New Testament at the Presbyterian Theological Seminary, Dubuque, Iowa, from 1953–55. From 1956–63 he held the position of Associate Professor of New Testament, Federated Theological Faculty, at the University of Chicago in Chicago, Illinois. In 1963 he became Professor of New Testament at the Pittsburgh Theological Seminary, Pittsburgh, Pennsylvania. Prof. Barth currently serves as an associate editor of the *Journal of Ecumenical Studies.*

Roland E. Murphy, Roman Catholic

Educational Background:

Ordained May 23, 1942.

About the Authors

S.T.D. and M.A., Catholic University of America, in Semitics.

Fellowship from the American Schools of Oriental Research for archeological work in Palestine (New Testament Jericho and Old Testament Dibon), 1950–1951.

S.S.L., Pontifical Biblical Institute, Rome, 1958.

Publications:

The Dead Sea Scrolls and the Bible, Westminster, Md., 1956.

Seven Books of Wisdom, Milwaukee, 1960.

Exodus, New York, 1960.

Catholic Biblical Quarterly, Editor in Chief.

Contributions to *Theological Studies, Biblica, Chicago Studies.*

Member of the editorial board of the Confraternity translation of the wisdom books of the Old Testament.

Other Pertinent Information:

In 1948 Father Murphy became instructor in the Department of Semitic languages at the Catholic University of America, and in 1956 entered the faculty of theology to teach Old Testament. Since 1945 he has taught Scripture at the Carmelite theologate, Whitefriars Hall, Washington, D.C. During these years Father Murphy has been active in summer biblical institutes for priests throughout the country, and has taught at summer sessions at the University of Notre Dame. This fall (1964) he is guest professor in Old Testament studies at Pittsburgh Theological Seminary (Presbyterian).

Steven S. Schwarzschild, Jewish

Educational Background:

B.A. in philosophy, University of Cincinnati.

Bachelor of Hebrew Letters, Master and Doctor of Hebrew

Letters, Hebrew Union College—Jewish Institute of Religion in Cincinnati.

Publications:

Judaism—A Quarterly Journal, Editor; sponsored by the American Jewish Congress, which is regarded as the most significant journal of Jewish religious thought in the world.
Franz Rosenzweig—Guide to Reversioners. London, 1962.
Articles contributed to *Hebrew Union College Annual, Yearbook of the Central Conference of American Rabbis, Conservative Judaism, Jewish Quarterly Review, Jewish Social Studies, Worldview,* . . .

Other Pertinent Information:

Rabbi Schwarzschild was rabbi of the Jewish Community of Berlin, Germany, and of the Federation of Jewish Communities in the Russian Occupation Zone, 1948–1950. In 1950 he became rabbi of Temple Beth El, Fargo, North Dakota, from whence, in 1957, he moved to become rabbi at Temple Beth El, Lynn, Massachusetts.

Rabbi Schwarzschild is the only American rabbi who is a member of both the (Reform) Central Conference of American Rabbis and of the (Conservative) Rabbinical Assembly of America and of important commissions of both. He has held office and still does in the Religion and Labor Foundation, the Jewish Peace Fellowship, Massachusetts Board of Rabbis, and many other organizations concerned with religious and social welfare. Dr. Schwarzschild has lectured at many academic and religious institutions, such as the Jewish Theological Seminary of America, Council on Religion and International Affairs, Harvard, Columbia, University of Pittsburgh. This year he has accepted a chair in Jewish studies at Brown University.

David Noel Freedman, Presbyterian

Educational Background:

UCLA, A.B., 1939 (History).
Princeton Theological Seminary, 1941–44, Th.B. (Old Testament).
Johns Hopkins University, 1945–48, Ph.D. (Semitic Languages and Literature).

Publications:

God Has Spoken. Philadelphia, 1949 (with J. D. Smart).
Early Hebrew Orthography. New Haven, 1952 (with F. M. Cross, Jr.).
The People of the Dead Sea Scrolls. New York, 1958 (with J. M. Allegro).
The Secret Sayings of Jesus. New York, 1960 (with R. M. Grant).

Articles:

Journal of Biblical Literature: '48, '53, '55, '58, '59.
Journal of Near Eastern Studies: '50, '52, '55.
Bulletin of the American Schools of Oriental Research: '47, '51, '58.
Biblical Archaeologist, 1956.
Interpretation, 1950, 1954.
Presbyterian Life (numerous items).
Zeitschrift fur die Alttestamentliche, 1953.
Western Watch (numerous items).
"The Pentateuch" in the *Interpreter's Dictionary of the Bible,* and other items.
"The Chronology of the Old Testament," in the *Albright Festschrift.* New York, 1960.
Hastings' One-Volume Dictionary of the Bible, revised ed., numerous items.

Other Pertinent Information:

Dr. Freedman was ordained to the ministry of the Presbyterian Church, USA, June 4, 1944. From 1946–47 he served as a teaching fellow at Johns Hopkins University, and then from 1947–48 as assistant instructor. The following three years Dr. Freedman was assistant professor of Old Testament at the Western Theological Seminary in Pittsburgh, and from 1951–60 was Professor of Hebrew and Old Testament Literature. With the formation of the Pittsburgh Theological Seminary in 1960, he held the position of Professor of Hebrew and Old Testament Literature.

From 1955–59 Dr. Freedman edited the *Journal of Biblical Literature.* In 1956 he became Associate Editor of the Anchor Bible Series. Presently Dr. Freedman serves as editorial consultant for the *Interpreter's Dictionary of the Bible* and for the Doubleday Book Company, Religious Book Department.

Anthony A. Stephenson, Roman Catholic

Education:

Wimbledon College (near London), 1917–26.
Exhibition to Christ's College, Cambridge, 1925.
Major Demyship to Magdalen College, Oxford, 1926. Neither taken up; became Jesuit.
Read 'Greats' (Litterae Humaniores) at Campion Hall, Oxford, 1931–35.
1st Cl., Hon. Moderations, 1933.
1st Cl., 'Greats,' 1935.
B.A., Oxon, 1935–36.
M.A., Oxon, 1938.
Professional studies (Scholastic Philosophy & Theology) at Heythrop College, Oxfordshire, 1928–31 and 1936–40.
S.T.L., Rome, by affiliation to Gregorian University.

About the Authors

Publications:

Articles contributed to *Clergy Review, Downside Review, Scrutiny, Theological Studies, Texte und Untersuchungen.*

Other Pertinent Information:

From 1959–63 Father Stephenson was a member of the Faculty of Theology at Oxford University where he lectured on The Jerusalem Mystagogical Catecheses and jointly conducted Roman-Angelican Orthodox Seminars. For the Spring Semester of 1963 he became visiting Professor at Loyola University, New Orleans (Theology). Then for 1963–64 Father Stephenson accepted a visiting professorship in the Department of Religion, McMaster University (Paul Rowntree Clifford Professor), Hamilton, Ontario.